Jensen Huang Biography

The Visionary Engineer Who Revolutionized AI and Gaming

The Way of NVIDIA (Innovation, Leadership, and the Future of Technology)

Theron Isaacson

GRAPEVINE BOOKS

Published by
GRAPEVINE BOOKS

www.grapevinebooks.com
email: grapevineindiapublishers@gmail.com

Ordering Information:
Quantity sales: Special discounts are available on quantity purchases by corporations, associations, and others.
For details, reach out to the publisher.

First published by Grapevine Books, 2025

Contents

Get Your Free Audiobook!

Scan the QR code below to instantly access the audiobook version of this book, absolutely free.

SCAN ME

Introduction

This is the story of a boy, who was working in the kitchen of Denny's. He was standing at the sink of a Denny's kitchen, scrubbing plates until his fingers wrinkled. The smell of grease clung to his clothes, the steam from the dish pit rising around him like a fog. He worked hard, not because he had to, but because he believed that every task, no matter how small, was worth doing well. "No one can carry more coffee cups than I can," he later joked.

Outside of work, he took on any job he could—cleaning floors, mopping bathrooms, bussing tables—never once complaining. He was an immigrant, a dreamer, a kid who didn't yet know what his future would hold. But he had one thing: an unshakable belief in learning, in curiosity, in building something greater.

Years later, that same boy—who once washed dishes just to get by—went on to co-found one of the biggest technology companies in the world, NVIDIA.

His name? Jensen Huang. The same Denny's where he worked, went onto because NVIDIA's first office. With no corporate office and no immediate funding, they did what many budding entrepreneurs have done before—they found the nearest place with free refills and a quiet corner to strategize. That place was a Denny's.

For months, the three men would meet in that booth, armed with notebooks, laptops, and an unwavering belief in their vision. The restaurant staff became familiar with their faces, watching as they scribbled down ideas, sketched out circuit designs, and debated the future of graphics technology over cups of coffee and plates of hash browns. Some of the most critical decisions about the company's early direction were made in that booth, fueled by caffeine and determination.

Despite their enthusiasm, securing funding was a monumental challenge. Investors were skeptical—graphics processing was considered a niche market at the time, with limited applications outside of video games. But Huang was persuasive. He had an innate ability to convey his vision in a way that made others believe in it, even if they didn't fully understand the technology. After relentless pitching and networking, NVIDIA managed to secure $40,000 in seed funding. It wasn't much, but it was enough to get started.

His journey is one of risk, sacrifice, and unwavering determination. His leadership philosophy—centered on technical skill, maximum effort, and an obsession with finding the best people—has placed him in the league of visionaries like Steve Jobs and Jeff Bezos. But what makes Jensen unique is not just his ability to build a great company, but his ability to teach, to inspire, and to shape those around him.

To understand Nvidia and its culture of excellence, one must first understand Jensen Huang. This biography explores not only his rise as a leader but also the principles that have guided his life—from his formative years to the struggles of founding Nvidia, and ultimately, to his role as a teacher and innovator. His journey is one of perseverance, of turning setbacks into stepping stones, and of never settling for anything less than greatness.

Before Nvidia became a powerhouse, before the world knew his name, there was a boy sent to America with little money, little understanding of the language, but an immeasurable drive to succeed.

This is his story.

Chapter 1: Origins and Early Life

Jensen Huang once recalled how, as a child, he admired a beautiful watch his father owned. It wasn't particularly expensive, but it had a metallic shine and a smooth ticking sound that fascinated him. One day, he asked his father if he could have it. His father smiled and said, "Work hard, and you can buy anything you want." It was a simple statement, but one that would shape Jensen's philosophy for the rest of his life.

Born in 1963 in Tainan, Taiwan, Jensen was raised in a humble yet intellectually curious family. His parents, both educators, emphasized the value of perseverance and knowledge. Taiwan, at the time, was undergoing rapid industrialization, but for most families, life was still defined by modest means and a strong work ethic. His parents worked tirelessly to provide for their children, instilling in Jensen a sense of discipline and ambition.

In Taiwan, Jensen lived in a small apartment with his family, where space was limited but imagination was boundless. One of his earliest memories was watching his mother carefully budget household expenses, writing down numbers in a notebook. "She could stretch a dollar like you wouldn't believe," he later said. It was in that cramped home that he first developed an appreciation for efficiency—something that would later translate into his obsession with optimizing technology.

As a child, he showed an early interest in how things worked. He would spend hours taking apart radios, fascinated by the intricate components inside. His curiosity was encouraged by his parents, who saw potential in his inquisitive nature. Despite financial constraints, they prioritized education, making sure their children had access to books and learning materials.

Jensen's uncle, who had moved to the United States, once sent a package from America. Inside were some candy bars and a small calculator—a device that Jensen had never seen before. He was mesmerized by how the calculator could perform complex functions with the press of a button. "I remember thinking, 'This thing is magic,'" he said. It was the first time he realized that technology could be powerful, and it sparked a deep curiosity that would later define his career.

At the age of four, Jensen's father left Taiwan for New York City, determined to lay the foundation for his family's future. Jensen and his brother, however, were not immediately brought along. Instead, they spent their early years in Taiwan, constantly moving as their father sought work and stability. Their mother, recognizing that her children would one day need to adapt to an

English-speaking world, took a unique approach to prepare them—every day, she would select ten words from the dictionary and make them memorize them.

This daily exercise was not just about learning English; it was about discipline, about persistence. And though Jensen could not have known it at the time, it was the beginning of a mindset that would define his entire life—the ability to endure discomfort and turn it into growth.

Leaving Home at Five

Jensen's parents, wanting a better future for their children, decided to send Jensen and his brother to live with their relatives in Thailand when he was just five years old. It was an incredibly difficult decision, but they believed it was the best path forward. At just five years old, in 1968, Jensen and his brother boarded a plane to Thailand without their parents.

The experience was terrifying—two young boys alone in a foreign country, adjusting to a new language and culture. "I cried myself to sleep many nights," he later admitted. But even at that age, he understood why his parents had sent him away.

In Thailand, Jensen lived with relatives and attended a local school. However, political instability and rising tensions in the country made his time there challenging. Despite the difficulties, the experience forced him to become independent at an early age. He learned to adapt quickly, a skill that would later help him navigate the fast-changing world of technology and business.

The first day of school in Thailand was a shock. Jensen had been sent to a boarding school in a small town without understanding the language or culture. He quickly realized that discipline there was enforced through strict punishments.

Once, after failing to complete a math assignment, he was sent to the principal's office, where he was punished with a wooden stick—a practice common in many Asian schools at the time. "I learned very quickly that I needed to survive," he later recalled.

He didn't let the experience break him. Instead, he found solace in numbers—math became his way of making sense of a world where everything else felt uncertain. It was in Thailand that he first developed the mental resilience that would define his leadership in the future.

The small apartment in which he lived with his relatives had a cracked window overlooking a busy street. Every evening, Jensen would sit by it, watching people pass by, imagining different futures. He often thought about his parents, wondering if they missed him as much as he missed them.

But something kept him going: the dream of going to America. His uncle had already moved there, and through letters, he described a world where "anything was possible." "I didn't know what the future held, but I knew I wanted to be part of that world," Jensen later said.

His parents finally secured an opportunity: Jensen and his brother would join their uncle in the United States. It was a life-changing decision, one that would set him on the path toward a world of innovation, computers, and ultimately, NVIDIA.

A Bus Ride to the Unknown

The journey to the U.S. began with a long bus ride through Thailand, followed by multiple flights. Jensen, now nine years old, still didn't fully understand the magnitude of the change. But as he looked out of the airplane window, watching the city lights fade beneath him, he felt a strange mix of excitement and fear.

When he landed in America, he expected to see towering skyscrapers and streets lined with golden opportunities. Instead, he found himself in rural Kentucky—a place far removed from the bustling cities of his imagination.

The reality of small-town America was stark: he and his brother lived with their uncle in a modest home, and adjusting to the culture was not easy. He barely spoke English, and school was once again a battle for survival.

But Jensen had learned something in Thailand—adaptation was key. If he could endure Thai boarding school, he could handle anything.

Jensen's early years in America were marked by challenges and small victories. He worked hard, mastering English while excelling in math and science. He had learned from his past experiences that hard work was the key to survival.

In many ways, immigrating to the U.S. was like rebooting his life. He wasn't just a kid from Taiwan anymore—he was someone who had lived through discipline in Thailand, isolation in Kentucky, and the uncertainty of change.

Jensen Huang had never seen snow before. Back in Taiwan and Thailand, winters were mild, but in Kentucky, it was different. One morning, he woke up to find the world outside completely white, the ground covered in a thick layer of snow.

Excited, he ran outside in his thin jacket, only to realize within seconds how brutally cold it was. His uncle laughed and handed him a second-hand winter coat. "Welcome to America," he said.

Jensen's first winter in rural Oneida, Kentucky, was not just about adjusting to the cold—it was about adjusting to an entirely new world. Unlike the bustling streets of Taiwan or the strict schools of Thailand, Oneida was quiet, remote, and isolated. For a boy who barely spoke English, life here would be both a challenge and a defining period of his life.

The Strange New School

The school wasn't like the ones he had attended before. Oneida Baptist Institute, where Jensen was enrolled, was a Christian boarding school with strict discipline. He had been sent there, not because he was a troublemaker, but because it was a place where immigrant children could receive an education while living far from home.

It didn't take long for him to realize that this was no ordinary school. Some of his classmates were there because they had disciplinary issues, and others because their parents couldn't afford to raise them. Jensen, on the other hand, was there simply to survive.

Jensen, smaller and younger than most of the students there, found himself in an environment that was as physically demanding as it was mentally challenging. His roommate was eight years older than him, covered in tattoos and scars, a stark contrast to the child who had just arrived from Taiwan. For the first few months, he was beaten up regularly, a harsh introduction to his new life.

But Jensen did not break. Instead, he adapted. He found his footing, earned respect, and learned an important lesson—resilience. Years later, reflecting on his time at Oneida, he would say, "I don't get scared often. I don't worry about going places I haven't gone before. I can tolerate a lot of discomfort." This was not just a reflection of his childhood; it was a preview of the kind of leader he would become.

The daily routine was rigorous: chores in the morning, classes during the day, and strict discipline at night. "There was no way out," he later said. "You followed the rules, or you faced the consequences."

One of the school's rules was that every student had to work. Jensen's first job was scrubbing floors and cleaning bathrooms. At first, he hated it, but then he realized something: if you were fast and efficient, you could finish your work early and have extra time to study or rest. So, he optimized everything—from the way he held the mop to the speed at which he finished his tasks. "I turned it into a game," he later said, laughing. "How fast could I clean a room without missing a spot?"

Looking back, he recognized that this experience shaped his obsession with efficiency and optimization—a mindset that would later influence how he built NVIDIA's groundbreaking technology.

First Times

For a long time, Jensen kept to himself. He barely spoke English, and in a school where many kids came from rough backgrounds, keeping a low profile was often the safest option.

One day, however, during a math class, the teacher asked a question that no one could answer. Jensen, who had always been strong in math, hesitated but then quietly raised his hand. "It's 144," he said.

The teacher nodded. "That's correct."

It was a small moment, but for Jensen, it was the first time he felt like he belonged. He realized that even if he struggled with language, he had a strength: numbers made sense, even when words didn't.

This quiet confidence in mathematics would later lead him to pursue engineering, ultimately setting him on the path to Stanford and NVIDIA.

There was a moment—one that Jensen never forgot—when he sat alone in his small dorm room, staring at the ceiling, wondering if this was all life had to offer.

He knew he was in a school filled with troubled kids, far from his parents, with an uncertain future ahead. But instead of feeling sorry for himself, he made a decision:

"I'm going to make something of myself."

That decision became his guiding force. He studied harder, worked faster, and adapted to his new world. When he eventually left Oneida Baptist Institute, he didn't just take memories—he took with him the resilience, discipline, and determination that would define his future.

Jensen was a teenager when he first laid hands on a real computer. It wasn't his—it belonged to a local university lab that allowed students to visit. The moment he saw the screen light up, his world changed.

The computer was slow, bulky, and required typing out long commands just to get it to do something simple. But to Jensen, it was the most powerful machine he had ever seen.

He spent hours trying to understand it, asking the lab technicians questions, and teaching himself the basics of programming. It felt like a new language, one he was desperate to master.

Later, he would describe this moment as his true turning point—the instant he realized that computers weren't just tools; they were the future.

Chapter 2: The Midnight Light in the Dorm Room

Jensen Huang's dorm room at Oregon State University was often the only one with a light on past midnight. His roommate would sometimes wake up in the middle of the night to see Jensen hunched over his desk, scribbling calculations or staring at a circuit board.

"Do you ever sleep?" his roommate once asked.

Jensen grinned. "Not when there's something interesting to figure out."

At Oregon State University (OSU), Jensen wasn't just studying engineering—he was living it. While other students took breaks after class, he would stay up late reading about semiconductors, circuits, and microprocessors, eager to understand the fundamentals of computing.

This was the start of his journey into the world of hardware and chip design, a passion that would later define his career.

The First Job Offer

During his time at OSU, Jensen worked on multiple side projects to sharpen his skills. He built circuits, programmed small devices, and studied how to make computer chips more efficient.

One day, a tech recruiter visited OSU, looking for young engineers with a deep understanding of microprocessors. Jensen, always eager to learn, asked dozens of questions about real-world chip design.

At the end of the conversation, the recruiter told him, "If you ever want a job, give me a call."

That was when Jensen realized that his knowledge wasn't just theoretical—it had real value in the industry. He had always been passionate about computers, but now he saw that he could build a career out of it.

After a long day of studying on an evening, Jensen took a walk around campus in the pouring Oregon rain.

As he walked, he thought about his journey—from Taiwan to Thailand to Kentucky, from scrubbing floors at a reform school to standing in a college classroom, designing circuits.

It hit him then: he had come so far, but this was just the beginning.

He wasn't studying electrical engineering just to get a degree—he wanted to build something that would change the future.

That night, as he dried off and sat at his desk, he made a promise to himself: "One day, I'm going to create something revolutionary."

And he would.

His first partnership

When Jensen Huang met his wife Lori Mills at Oregon State University, the odds weren't in his favor. He was 17 years old, and she was 19. "I was the youngest kid in school, in class. There were 250 students and 3 girls," he said in an interview at the Hong Kong University of Science and Technology after receiving an honorary degree. He was also the only student who "looked like a child."

Huang used his youthful appearance to approach his future wife, hoping she would assume he was smart. "I walked up to her and I said, 'Do you want to see my homework?'" Then he made a deal with her. "If you do homework with me every Sunday, I promise you, you will get straight As."

From that point on, he had a date every Sunday. And just to ensure that she would eventually marry him, he made her another promise: by 30, he would be a CEO.

Their partnership grew naturally, built on mutual respect and admiration. They worked together on various projects, spending countless hours in the lab. Lori's approach to problem-solving complemented Jensen's, and they found that they made a strong team both academically and personally. Over time, their professional collaboration deepened into a personal connection.

After graduating from Oregon State, Jensen continued his education at Stanford University, while Lori remained a steadfast presence in his life. Their relationship endured through these transitions, and five years after meeting, they married. According to his biography on OSU College of Engineering's website, they later had two children: Madison, who became a director of marketing at Nvidia, and Spencer, who works as a senior product manager at the company.

Lori played a significant role in Jensen's journey, providing him with stability and support as he navigated the challenges of building his career. Throughout his ascent in the tech industry, she remained a grounding influence, offering encouragement as he co-founded Nvidia and led it to become one of the world's most influential technology companies.

Jensen Huang didn't live like most Stanford graduate students. While some of his classmates had comfortably funded education, Jensen was on a tight budget. He often ate the same meal every day: a $2.50 burrito from a local taqueria.

A friend once asked him, "Why don't you eat something different?"

Jensen laughed. "Because burritos are efficient—just like a good chip design."

His time at Stanford wasn't just about high-level computing theories—it was about learning how to do more with less. In both life and engineering, he believed that efficiency and optimization were everything. This philosophy would later influence his groundbreaking work at NVIDIA, where he focused on making computing faster, cheaper, and more powerful.

Stanford's Center for Integrated Systems was where the best minds in chip design worked, and Jensen spent most of his waking hours there. One night, around 2 AM, a professor walked in and found Jensen still working at his station, deep in thought over a complex circuit design problem.

The professor chuckled. "You do know Stanford has dorms, right?"

Jensen grinned, "Why sleep when I can figure this out?"

He was obsessed—not just with learning, but with understanding computing at its deepest level. Stanford wasn't just another degree for him—it was a launchpad into the future of technology.

The First Real Glimpse of the Future

During his master's program, Jensen worked with cutting-edge semiconductor technology, studying how to make processors more efficient.

One day, while testing parallel processing techniques, he had a realization: "Computers should think like the human brain—many things happening at once, not just one step at a time."

This idea of parallel computing would later become the foundation of NVIDIA's GPU revolution. But at the time, it was just a fascination with making computers smarter and faster.

What he didn't know was that this insight would change the future of artificial intelligence decades later.

While sitting in the engineering library, one afternoon, Jensen got a call from LSI Logic, a semiconductor company. They had heard about his work and wanted to offer him a full-time engineering job—before he had even graduated. It was a tough decision. Should he finish his master's degree or jump straight into the industry?

Jensen, always valuing practical experience over theory, decided to take the job while completing his degree at night. He worked during the day, studied at night, and pushed himself to the absolute limit.

From Toilet Scrubber to Tech Pioneer

Jensen Huang stood at a crossroads early in his career when he received offers from both AMD and LSI Logic. He chose AMD, the company he had admired since seeing their microprocessor poster during his college days. There, he designed microchips while simultaneously pursuing his master's degree in electrical engineering at Stanford and raising two children with his wife Lori. His dedication to completing his degree over eight years revealed his character: "I have a very long-term horizon. I can be impatient about certain things, but infinitely patient about others. I plug away."

Despite achieving the immigrant family dream—securing an excellent education and career in America—Jensen's ambition pushed him further. He grew frustrated with the tedious, manual process of designing microchips at AMD. When he heard that LSI Logic was pioneering new software tools that would revolutionize chip design, he faced a difficult choice: remain in his secure position or risk everything for innovation.

His forward-thinking nature prevailed. He took "the plunge" and joined LSI, where he was assigned to work with Sun Microsystems. There, he met engineers Curtis Priem and Chris Malachowsky, who were developing technology that would transform workstation computers.

While luck and talent played roles in his journey from scrubbing toilets to managing divisions at a microchip company, Jensen attributed his success primarily to his exceptional work ethic and resilience: "People with very high expectations have very low resilience. Unfortunately, resilience matters in success. Greatness is not intelligence. Greatness comes from character." In his view, character could only develop through overcoming adversity.

This philosophy explained why, when asked for advice on achieving success,

Jensen consistently replied: "I wish upon you ample doses of pain and suffering."

The Meeting That Made Him Stay Late

Jensen Huang had been working at LSI Logic for just a few months when he was invited to sit in on a high-level strategy meeting. At first, he wasn't sure why he was there—he was just a young engineer. But as the executives debated the future of semiconductors, he listened intently. One executive laid out the problem: chip performance was increasing, but the demand for computing power was growing even faster.

Jensen stayed late that night, sketching out his own solutions on a whiteboard in his office. He wasn't just interested in how semiconductors worked—he wanted to know how they could be made better. That night, he realized: this industry wasn't just about designing chips—it was about solving the impossible.

One afternoon, Jensen had lunch with a senior engineer at LSI Logic, who had spent decades in the semiconductor industry. The engineer leaned in and said:

"Do you know what's coming, Jensen? The world is going to need more computing power than ever before. But CPUs won't be enough."

Jensen listened carefully, absorbing every word. The idea stuck with him—was there another way to handle massive computing workloads?

Years later, this conversation would influence his decision to develop GPUs—not just for gaming, but for parallel processing, AI, and high-performance computing.

At the time, he didn't know how it would happen. But he knew it would happen.

Jensen once visited a state-of-the-art semiconductor fabrication plant while working in the industry. As he walked through the facility, watching robotic arms move wafers with extreme precision, he was mesmerized.

He asked one of the engineers, "How much does it cost to build one of these plants?"

The engineer laughed. "Billions."

Jensen was stunned. He had always known that the semiconductor business was expensive, but seeing it firsthand made him understand why only a few companies could compete.

That visit cemented a belief that stayed with him: semiconductors were the heart of computing, and whoever controlled computing power controlled the future.

In the late 1980s, Jensen attended a semiconductor and computing trade show, where the industry's biggest companies showcased their latest technology.

He walked past Intel's booth, where they were showing off their newest CPU. He saw IBM's workstation computers, massive but powerful. And then he stumbled across a small booth showcasing graphics chips for video games.

That was the moment when he saw it: graphics computing was advancing, but no one was taking it seriously as a computing solution beyond gaming.

"What if graphics chips could do more?" he thought. "What if they could power AI, simulations, and scientific computing?"

Years later, this exact thought would lead to the creation of NVIDIA's first GPU, a chip that would revolutionize computing forever.

Chapter 3: The Birth of Geniuses

When LSI Logic assigned Jensen Huang to manage the Sun Microsystems account, he had no idea he was stepping into history. Fresh from AMD, he was eager to prove himself, but the two engineers he met - Curtis Priem and Chris Malachowsky - were unlike anyone he'd worked with before.

In a small high school in Fairview Park, Ohio, a teenaged Curtis Priem discovered his passion in the glow of a Teletype Model 33 terminal. Connected to a distant mainframe by a sluggish phone line, he taught himself programming by creating games in BASIC.

His masterpiece was a text-based billiards simulation. Players would input angles and speeds, and the mainframe would calculate collisions and new positions of the balls. The program was so massive that its punched tape roll grew to nearly nine inches in diameter, requiring almost an hour to print each new version. When he entered it in a local science fair, it earned him first prize. His first graphics experimentation—scaling and rotating a digitized photo of his Mathematics teacher himself—planted the seeds for what would eventually become groundbreaking work in computer graphics.

Chris Malachowsky's turning point was no less unique. When he aced the electrical section of his physics class, he barely gave it a second thought. It wasn't until he lay on a picnic table during the lunch break of his MCAT exam, squinting up at the bright Florida sun, that doubt crept in. As he contemplated the reality of a physician's life - the endless on-call hours, the sleep deprivation, the pharmaceutical minutiae - a simple question formed in his mind: "Do I really want to know what all the names on drug bottles mean?"

The answer came with surprising clarity: "No. I like this engineering stuff. I'd rather be an engineer."

After completing the exam, he stopped only to grab a case of beer at 7-Eleven before rushing home to call his parents with what he assumed would be disappointing news.

"Mom, Dad, I've got good news and bad news," he told them nervously. "The good news is the test wasn't that hard. The bad news is, I don't want to be a doctor anymore."

He braced for their disappointment, but instead heard relief in his mother's voice.

"Good," she said. "You never read directions anyway. We didn't think you'd be a good one. We thought you were doing it for your father."

With his parents' unexpected blessing, Malachowsky pursued electrical engineering instead.

What began as a practice interview changed Chris Malachowsky's life forever. Despite having no graphics experience, his curiosity led him to meet with Curtis Priem at Sun Microsystems. Their complementary skills formed an immediate connection - Curtis understood graphics theory, while Chris excelled at practical implementation.

Curtis had designed an ambitious graphics accelerator with two dedicated ASICs that could handle 80% of computational workload, freeing up the CPU. But turning this theoretical marvel into reality required expertise beyond Sun's capabilities.

Enter LSI Logic, the leader in custom ASIC fabrication. With their new "sea-of-gates" architecture, LSI could fit over ten thousand gate arrays on a single chip - though Curtis's designs would push even these boundaries. LSI recognized the enormous potential of Sun's business and assigned their rising star, Jensen Huang, to manage the relationship.

This created the perfect trio: Curtis provided the visionary graphics expertise, Chris brought practical engineering know-how, and Jensen bridged the gap between ambitious design and manufacturing reality. Their combined talents - imagination, practicality, and technical problem-solving - would prove an unbeatable combination, setting the stage for a revolution in computer graphics.

So Curtis was the visionary, the graphics genius who designed this monstrous accelerator with two dedicated ASICs: the frame buffer controller and the transformation engine. His design was ambitious - offloading 80% of the computational workload from the CPU to dedicated graphics chips. Impressive on paper, but could it be built?

That's where Chris came in - the practical problem-solver. While Curtis dreamed in pixels and processors, Chris wrestled with implementation. He needed LSI's cutting-edge "sea-of-gates" technology to fit more than ten thousand gate arrays onto a single chip.

Jensen's job? Bridge the gap between Curtis's ambitious designs, Chris's pragmatic engineering, and LSI's manufacturing capabilities. As he helped them navigate the complexities of custom chip fabrication, Jensen found himself drawn into their vision. They weren't just building graphics cards - they were reimagining computing itself. Chris Malachowsky and Curtis

Priem shared his vision. They had an idea about the future of computing, one that involved harnessing the power of graphics chips for more than just video games. It was an idea that had never been fully realized before, and it was risky. But risk did not scare Jensen. What mattered was the challenge.

And somehow, he knew this partnership would lead to something extraordinary.

Clash of Brilliance

"No, that's not going to work!" Curtis Priem's voice echoed through the Sun Microsystems office as he slammed his palm on the table. Across from him, Chris Malachowsky's face reddened, his own frustration mounting.

"If you'd just listen for one minute," Chris shot back, "you'd understand why we need to approach it this way!"

This sort of shouting match was typical of the trio. Curtis, the graphics genius whose mind leaped from problem to solution with dizzying speed, struggled to articulate the complex architecture forming in his imagination. Chris, the practical engineer, fought to extract the critical technical specifications needed to actually build the thing.

"We can't fit that many gates on the chip! It's physically impossible!" Chris yelled, throwing his hands up.

"Then find a way to make it possible!" Curtis thundered before storming out of the room, leaving a stunned silence behind him.

Tom Webber and Vitus Leung, the other hardware engineers on the team, exchanged worried glances. Someone finally asked the question everyone was thinking: "Is this it? Is the team finished?"

Chris took a deep breath and smiled. "We're good," he said calmly, as if nothing unusual had happened. "He just gave me exactly what I needed to know."

"Curtis is so bright. He thinks so fast," Malachowsky later explained. "He starts with an idea and jumps to a solution and there are no breadcrumbs between the two. I really felt that my biggest contribution was helping him articulate [his ideas] for other people in a way that they could get behind. My communication skills turned out to be equally important as my engineering skills."

Jensen quickly recognized that their argumentative process was actually a crucible for innovation. These men were pushing boundaries that no one had dared approach before, developing a graphics accelerator that would revolutionize computing.

"We broke every tool that LSI Logic had in their standard portfolio," recalled Malachowsky. The specifications they needed - a frame buffer controller with 43,000 gates and 170,000 transistors, and a transformation engine requiring 25,000 gates and 212,000 transistors - were unprecedented.

Lesser engineers might have balked, but Jensen embraced the challenge. "Jensen was bright enough and savvy enough to say, 'Look, I'll fix these problems at the back end. You can ignore them. These you'd better fix because I don't know if I can handle those.'"

By 1989, the three men had accomplished what many thought impossible, finalizing the specifications for Sun's revolutionary "GX graphics engine." Their creation would handle up to 80 percent of computational workload independently, freeing the CPU for other tasks - a breakthrough that would transform both workstation performance and the future of graphics processing.

Their success was all the more remarkable given that they'd operated in secret, defying direct orders. Earlier, Sun executive Bernie Lacroute had explicitly forbidden resources for graphics development. When he eventually asked Wayne Rosing if he had followed this order, Rosing truthfully answered "no."

To everyone's surprise, Lacroute responded with one word: "Good."

The executive had recognized what the trio instinctively understood - that graphics would become critical to computing's future. What began as a clandestine "closet graphics" project emerged as Sun's competitive advantage in the workstation market.

Jensen saw those heated arguments not as dysfunction but as crucial to their success. He called them examples of "honing the sword." Just as a sword only becomes sharper when it meets grinding resistance, the best ideas always seemed to come from spirited debate and argument, even if the back-and-forth could get uncomfortable.

In those intense, sometimes uncomfortable confrontations, Jensen witnessed firsthand how different perspectives, forcefully defended, could yield extraordinary results. He saw more promise than peril in these explosive fights - a philosophy of embracing productive conflict that would eventually define his leadership at NVIDIA, the company these three would later found together.

What appeared to outsiders as chaos was actually the necessary friction of genius at work - the spark that would ignite a graphics revolution.

The Capacity for Pain

When Curtis and Chris decided to leave Sun Microsystems to start their own company, they initially approached Jensen for business advice. But as they worked together, the idea became clear—why work for someone else when they could build something themselves? Jensen, seeing the opportunity before him, didn't hesitate.

But starting a company required more than just an idea. It required funding. And this is where Jensen's reputation played a crucial role. When he approached the CEO of LSI Logic, Wilfred Corrigan, to inform him of his departure, Corrigan's first response wasn't to dissuade him. Instead, he asked, "Can I invest?"

Corrigan then introduced Jensen to Don Valentine, the legendary venture capitalist behind Sequoia Capital. Jensen's pitch to Valentine was, by his own admission, terrible. He couldn't clearly articulate what he was building, who it was for, or why it would succeed. And yet, at the end of the meeting, Valentine decided to invest anyway.

Why?

Because of Jensen's reputation. His work ethic, his intelligence, and his ability to endure hardship spoke louder than his words.

As Jensen himself later reflected, "We succeeded on the strength of our reputation, not our business plan."

Jensen's rise was not smooth. The early days of Nvidia were marked by failures, setbacks, and moments where the company nearly collapsed. But he had already built within himself the endurance to withstand pain. He had learned at Oneida how to take a beating and come back stronger. He had learned at Stanford how to work for years without immediate results. He had learned at AMD and LSI Logic how to keep pushing, no matter the difficulty.

This resilience became the foundation of his leadership. He demanded the same level of endurance from his team, believing that excellence is the capacity to take pain.

When he looks back at his journey, Jensen does not shy away from the difficulties. Instead, he embraces them, recognizing that every hardship prepared him for the road ahead.

And as Nvidia began its ascent, those early lessons—the ones formed in the dorm rooms of a reform school, the late nights at Stanford, the grueling years in the industry—became the very principles that would guide the company into the future.

Jensen Huang had built not just a company, but a legacy—one that was born out of struggle, shaped by discipline, and defined by an unbreakable will to succeed.

However, as Jensen's career progressed and his responsibilities at Nvidia grew, their marriage eventually came to an end. Though the details of their separation remain private, it marked a significant chapter in his personal life. Despite the changes, both Jensen and Lori continued their individual paths, with their legacy together remaining evident in their shared history and their children's roles in the family business.

Their story is one of partnership, built on trust, respect, and shared ambitions. Lori's presence in Jensen's life was integral to his success, demonstrating that personal support and professional drive can coexist, even as life takes different turns.

Chapter 4: Building the Future Before It Exists

Jensen Huang never set out to merely compete. He was not interested in chasing market share in existing industries, nor was he content with iterative progress. Instead, his philosophy was simple but radical: create new markets rather than compete in them. This approach would define Nvidia's trajectory, transforming it from a struggling startup into a trillion-dollar tech behemoth.

This idea—that the greatest opportunities lie not in refining existing technologies but in inventing entirely new fields—was present from the very beginning of his journey. It was a belief forged in his early struggles, his relentless pursuit of excellence, and a deep understanding of the technological currents shaping the future. Jensen didn't want to play the game—he wanted to write the rules.

The Early Days

In the 1990s, the semiconductor industry was a battlefield. Companies were fiercely competing to produce the fastest processors, more efficient memory, and cost-effective microchips. It was an industry driven by incremental gains, with every player attempting to shave milliseconds off computing times or squeeze more transistors onto a chip.

But Jensen saw something else.

He saw that computing was not just about speed—it was about possibility. Traditional CPUs were improving, but their fundamental architecture limited their ability to handle complex, parallel processing tasks. Jensen believed the future of computing wasn't about making general-purpose processors slightly better; it was about rethinking the entire way computers worked. He envisioned a world where visual computing, artificial intelligence, and high-performance parallel processing would shape the next revolution.

This was a radical departure from conventional thinking. When Nvidia was founded in 1993, few believed in the power of graphics processing units (GPUs) beyond their use in gaming. Companies like Intel dominated the market, and most investors saw no need for an entirely new category of processors. But Jensen was unwavering.

He bet Nvidia's future on the idea that GPUs would become the most essential computing tools in the world.

Initially, Nvidia's survival depended on making GPUs viable for gaming. In 1999, the company launched the GeForce 256, the world's first graphics processing unit (GPU). While other companies were dabbling in 3D acceleration, Nvidia was the first to fully commit to the idea that GPUs could completely revolutionize the gaming experience.

Jensen wasn't just competing with existing graphics cards; he was creating an entirely new demand. He understood that gamers didn't just want better graphics—they wanted immersion, realism, and performance that felt limitless. The launch of the GeForce series marked the beginning of an era where GPUs became indispensable for gaming.

The decision to bet on GPUs for gaming paid off handsomely. Within a few years, Nvidia was synonymous with high-performance graphics, and gaming became a multi-billion-dollar industry. But for Jensen, gaming was just the first step. He wasn't content with merely dominating an industry—he was searching for the next frontier.

Beyond Gaming

Even as Nvidia was enjoying its success in gaming, Jensen was already thinking several steps ahead. He saw an opportunity where few others did: scientific computing, artificial intelligence, and deep learning.

The traditional CPU-centric approach to computing was limiting researchers and developers. Jensen knew that Nvidia's parallel computing architecture could solve problems at a scale that traditional processors never could. He envisioned a future where GPUs would power medical research, weather forecasting, financial modeling, and even artificial intelligence.

In 2006, Nvidia introduced CUDA (Compute Unified Device Architecture), a revolutionary framework that allowed developers to use GPUs for general-purpose computing. CUDA transformed GPUs from niche gaming tools into powerful accelerators for data-intensive computing.

Most of the world didn't realize it yet, but Jensen had just built the foundation for AI and deep learning.

Betting on the Next Revolution

In the early 2010s, artificial intelligence was still largely confined to research labs. The computational power required to train neural networks was astronomical, and few believed it could ever be practical on a large scale. But once again, Jensen was ahead of the curve.

He understood that deep learning wasn't just another technological trend—it was the future of computing itself. He also knew that Nvidia's GPUs were uniquely suited for the kind of matrix-heavy computations that deep learning required. Where others saw an experimental field, Jensen saw the next great technological revolution.

While tech giants like Google, Microsoft, and Facebook were beginning to explore AI, Jensen went all-in. Nvidia shifted its entire strategy toward becoming the backbone of artificial intelligence. He spearheaded the development of AI-focused GPUs like the Tesla V100, ensuring that Nvidia's hardware would be at the heart of every major AI breakthrough.

The bet paid off in spectacular fashion. By the mid-2010s, every major AI breakthrough—from self-driving cars to natural language processing—was powered by Nvidia's GPUs. Jensen had once again created a market before anyone else realized it existed.

As AI adoption grew, companies needed massive computational power to train and deploy machine learning models. Jensen recognized that Nvidia could not only provide the hardware but dominate the infrastructure layer of AI computing.

Under his leadership, Nvidia expanded aggressively into data centers, providing GPUs that powered cloud-based AI services. In 2020, the company acquired Arm Holdings, a move that positioned Nvidia as a central player in the future of computing across mobile, cloud, and AI platforms.

By the 2020s, Nvidia was no longer just a gaming company. It was the foundation of AI, autonomous vehicles, robotics, and high-performance computing.

The Legacy of Market Creation

Jensen's success was not about winning in competitive markets—it was about creating them before anyone else saw their potential.

His method was simple:

- Identify an industry bottleneck – Find where existing solutions are failing.

- Rethink the problem from first principles – Question everything about how the problem is being solved today.

- Bet big before anyone else does – Invest resources into the new market before competitors even recognize its existence.

- Create a platform, not just a product – Build ecosystems (CUDA, AI GPUs, cloud infrastructure) that become indispensable.

- Scale aggressively – Once adoption starts, move fast and capture market dominance.

Jensen Huang's story is not just about technology—it's about vision and execution. Where others fought to be slightly better, he redefined the playing field. He saw what computing could be decades before the world caught up, and he built Nvidia into a company that did not just follow technological revolutions but led them.

Today, Nvidia's GPUs power AI research, self-driving cars, and data centers across the world. And yet, if history is any indication, Jensen is likely already thinking about the next market to create.

For Jensen Huang, the question has never been, "How do we win?"

The question has always been, "What comes next?"

Chapter 5: The 10-Minute Decision That Changed Everything

Some business decisions take months of planning, analysis, and endless debates. Others are made in the blink of an eye—but their impact lasts for decades. For Jensen Huang, the co-founder and CEO of NVIDIA, one such moment came when he made a 10-minute decision that would ultimately transform NVIDIA from a leading graphics company into the backbone of the artificial intelligence revolution. That decision? Making CUDA, NVIDIA's revolutionary AI and GPU computing platform, open and free for developers.

In the early 2000s, NVIDIA was primarily known for its dominance in gaming graphics. GPUs had been used almost exclusively for rendering video game visuals, and while they had proven themselves as powerful computing tools, they were still largely confined to the world of entertainment. However, Huang and his team saw a different potential. They believed GPUs could be used for far more than just graphics—specifically, they could power complex scientific calculations, deep learning models, and AI research.

This led to the development of CUDA (Compute Unified Device Architecture), a parallel computing platform and API that allowed developers to harness the massive processing power of GPUs for a variety of tasks beyond gaming. The platform was groundbreaking, but it faced a crucial challenge: adoption. Would developers actually use it?

Internally, the NVIDIA leadership team debated whether they should charge for CUDA access. Some executives feared that giving away such a powerful tool for free would mean losing out on valuable revenue. Others argued that if CUDA remained a proprietary, closed system, it might struggle to gain widespread adoption. The concern was that if NVIDIA locked down the platform, developers might simply ignore it and seek alternatives.

In a high-stakes meeting, the discussion raged on. Some executives wanted to charge licensing fees. Others wanted a subscription model. Arguments were presented, counterpoints raised, and concerns voiced. Then, after listening to both sides, Huang made a decision in just 10 minutes.

"Do it," he said. "Make it free."

With those three words, Huang changed NVIDIA's trajectory forever. By making CUDA open and accessible, he ensured that developers, researchers, and AI scientists around the world could use NVIDIA's hardware without financial barriers. This single decision made NVIDIA's GPUs the go-to platform for deep learning and artificial intelligence.

Once CUDA was freely available, developers began flocking to it. Universities started incorporating it into their AI research, data scientists used it to train complex neural networks, and companies realized they could leverage NVIDIA GPUs for everything from self-driving cars to drug discovery. By lowering the barriers to entry, Huang had essentially ensured that an entire generation of AI pioneers would build their technology on NVIDIA's platform.

The timing couldn't have been better. In 2012, a breakthrough AI model called AlexNet, powered by NVIDIA GPUs, won the ImageNet competition, proving that deep learning could outperform traditional machine learning approaches. From that moment on, the AI boom accelerated, and NVIDIA was at the center of it all.

Fast forward to today, and NVIDIA is valued at over $1 trillion. AI companies worldwide—from OpenAI to Tesla—depend on NVIDIA's technology. The decision to make CUDA free didn't just create a thriving developer ecosystem; it cemented NVIDIA's dominance in AI and high-performance computing. Without CUDA's widespread adoption, the AI revolution might have taken a very different path.

Reflecting on the decision, Huang later remarked, "Sometimes, the best way to win is to give something away. If you build the foundation for innovation, people will come."

It was a gamble. It was a risk. But in the end, it was a 10-minute decision that changed everything.

Jensen Huang has always been known for his ability to see the future before others do. He doesn't just follow trends—he creates them. In an industry where proprietary technology is often guarded like a state secret, Huang took a radically different approach. Instead of hoarding NVIDIA's AI software stack, he made the decision to give it away for free, an unprecedented move that ultimately solidified NVIDIA's dominance in artificial intelligence.

In the early days of AI development, many companies focused on building closed ecosystems, keeping their software proprietary and limiting access to their technology. The logic was simple: control the tools, control the market. But Huang saw a different path. He understood that for AI to reach its full potential, it needed collaboration on a massive scale. Developers, researchers, and engineers worldwide had to be able to build upon existing work rather than starting from scratch. If NVIDIA made its AI software open-source, it would create a new paradigm—one where innovation was accelerated, and

NVIDIA became the default infrastructure of AI.

This decision was not without risk. At the time, NVIDIA was already a leader in AI hardware, thanks to its CUDA-enabled GPUs. Making its AI software freely available meant that competitors could access the same powerful tools. But Huang wasn't concerned about competition in the traditional sense. He wasn't playing a zero-sum game; he was expanding the playing field altogether. By giving away software, NVIDIA ensured that its hardware remained essential. After all, what good is a powerful AI software suite if it runs best on NVIDIA's GPUs?

NVIDIA's AI software stack includes frameworks like TensorRT for deep learning inference, cuDNN for neural network acceleration, and RAPIDS for data science. These tools drastically reduce the time it takes for AI models to be trained and deployed. By making them open-source, Huang ensured that developers around the world would standardize their AI workloads on NVIDIA's platform. It was a long-term strategy aimed at making NVIDIA indispensable in the AI ecosystem.

One of the biggest impacts of this decision was the acceleration of AI innovation. Researchers no longer had to worry about access to expensive proprietary software. Startups could leverage NVIDIA's technology without massive upfront costs, allowing them to focus on breakthroughs rather than infrastructure. Universities and research institutions began using NVIDIA's software stack to teach the next generation of AI engineers, further cementing the company's place at the heart of the AI revolution.

This strategy also helped NVIDIA form deep relationships with companies across industries. AI wasn't just about academia or startups anymore—it was being integrated into everything from healthcare to finance to autonomous vehicles. NVIDIA's software became the backbone of AI research in major corporations, including Tesla for self-driving cars, Google for cloud-based AI, and OpenAI for models like ChatGPT. Even competitors like AMD and Intel had to adopt NVIDIA's standards simply because the ecosystem was too powerful to ignore.

By the time AI truly exploded in the 2020s, NVIDIA was already years ahead. The move to open-source its AI stack had not only democratized access to powerful AI tools but also ensured that NVIDIA's hardware remained the gold standard for high-performance computing. Instead of fearing imitation, Huang embraced it, knowing that widespread adoption of NVIDIA's software meant even greater demand for its GPUs.

Jensen Huang's decision to give away NVIDIA's AI software for free wasn't just about generosity—it was a calculated move that reshaped the industry.

It ensured that NVIDIA would be at the center of AI's evolution, not just as a hardware provider, but as an ecosystem builder. While other companies focused on short-term gains, Huang played the long game, and in doing so, secured NVIDIA's place as the backbone of artificial intelligence for decades to come.

Relentless Execution

Jensen Huang was never one for half-measures. If there was one quality that defined his leadership at Nvidia more than any other, it was his unrelenting focus on execution. While ideas were abundant in Silicon Valley, execution was what separated the truly transformative companies from those that remained stuck in potential. To Jensen, execution wasn't just about getting things done; it was about getting things done the right way, at the right time, with the right people. His philosophy was simple yet profound: ideas are worthless without execution.

The Foundation of an Execution-Driven Mindset

From the earliest days of Nvidia, Jensen understood that great ideas were necessary but insufficient. What mattered was the ability to turn those ideas into tangible products, services, and market dominance. His rigorous discipline around execution was not a learned behavior—it was intrinsic to his very nature.

As a young engineer, working his way through the ranks of Advanced Micro Devices (AMD) and LSI Logic, Jensen was struck by how many promising projects failed due to a lack of disciplined follow-through. He noticed that many engineers, despite their brilliance, were content with conceptual brilliance rather than practical implementation. That realization shaped his philosophy: greatness wasn't about intelligence alone; it was about relentless persistence, iteration, and delivery.

When he co-founded Nvidia in 1993 with Curtis Priem and Chris Malachowsky, the company had no room for failure. They were up against giants like Intel, who had vast resources, deep industry ties, and the ability to outspend any startup into oblivion. Nvidia's only advantage was speed and execution. If they weren't the first to market with their innovations, they would be irrelevant.

The Nvidia Way: Speed, Precision, and Accountability

Jensen's leadership created what came to be known as The Nvidia Way—an ethos built around extreme accountability and a refusal to tolerate inefficiency. Nvidia's culture did not allow for the slow, bureaucratic decision-making processes that plagued larger corporations. Instead, Jensen installed a flat organizational structure where the best ideas could rise to the top quickly, and execution could begin without layers of approvals.

One of his most radical approaches was his stance on direct reports and one-on-one meetings—or rather, the lack of them. Unlike traditional CEOs who maintained a handful of direct reports and relied on cascading layers of management, Jensen chose to have over 60 direct reports. The reason? Speed. He wanted to hear information firsthand, make decisions instantly, and ensure that no unnecessary bureaucracy slowed Nvidia down.

Additionally, Nvidia meetings were structured around whiteboarding and real-time problem-solving rather than long PowerPoint presentations. Ideas were expected to be sketched out and debated live, forcing employees to think on their feet and drive toward execution rather than getting lost in theoretical discussions. The whiteboard became a symbol of Nvidia's culture—everything was up for iteration, refinement, and, if necessary, erasure. There was no room for complacency.

Execution as a Competitive Advantage

One of the most striking examples of Nvidia's execution-driven culture was the development of the GeForce 256, the world's first graphics processing unit (GPU). When the concept of the GPU was first proposed, Nvidia was still a young company, struggling to establish itself in a field dominated by better-funded competitors.

Most companies would have taken years to develop the technology and bring it to market. But Jensen refused to let Nvidia fall into that trap. Instead, he set an aggressive timeline, pushing his team beyond what they thought was possible.

The first attempt at creating a cutting-edge graphics chip, the NV1, had been a failure. It was a lesson that Jensen never forgot. Rather than retreating or slowing down after a major failure, Nvidia doubled down on execution, ensuring that every mistake was treated as a learning opportunity rather than a setback.

Jensen implemented weekly execution reviews, where engineers were required to present exactly what progress had been made, what obstacles were encountered, and how they were being addressed. There was no tolerance for excuses. Either progress was made, or it wasn't. This obsessive focus on execution allowed Nvidia to launch the GeForce 256 in 1999, revolutionizing the graphics industry and cementing Nvidia's place as a market leader.

The Pain of Execution: No Shortcuts, No Excuses

Jensen's philosophy on execution was not for the faint of heart. He demanded more from his employees than most leaders—not because he wanted to be harsh, but because he believed that true excellence required endurance.

His mantra was clear: "Excellence is the capacity to take pain."

For Jensen, execution wasn't about working harder—it was about working smarter and faster. Nvidia engineers often recalled how Jensen would visit their workstations unannounced, ask difficult questions, and expect immediate, well-thought-out answers. If a problem had been identified but not yet solved, he expected a clear plan of action for resolving it. "If you can't explain how you're going to fix it," he often said, "you haven't thought hard enough about the problem."

When Nvidia embarked on its AI revolution in the 2010s, this relentless focus on execution became even more critical. Jensen foresaw the role of GPUs in artificial intelligence long before most of the industry did. But vision alone wasn't enough—Nvidia had to execute faster than anyone else. They had to build the AI computing ecosystem before the world realized it needed one.

The Cost of Relentless Execution

Jensen's execution philosophy also came with a cost. Nvidia was not an easy place to work. The intensity of expectations meant that those who weren't prepared to give their best found themselves quickly out of place. Turnover was high, and employees either thrived under pressure or burned out.

But those who stayed and embraced the Nvidia Way often found themselves transformed. Jensen's approach bred an elite culture—one where the best minds in engineering, AI, and computing came together to push the boundaries of what was possible.

One Nvidia executive put it best: "Working with Jensen is like training with an Olympic coach. It's grueling, but if you survive, you come out world-class."

Execution in the Age of AI

As Nvidia expanded its dominance beyond gaming and into AI, Jensen's principles of execution remained unchanged. While other companies debated the future of AI computing, Nvidia built it. They developed CUDA, the parallel computing platform that became the foundation for deep learning. They built AI supercomputers, invested in self-driving car technology, and expanded into data centers, robotics, and healthcare AI.

Every step of the way, execution was the differentiator. When Jensen saw that AI was about to explode, Nvidia didn't just invest in AI chips; they built an entire AI computing ecosystem, from hardware to software to research collaborations.

This was the essence of Jensen's philosophy. Anyone could predict trends, but only a few could execute fast enough to dominate them.

The Legacy of Relentless Execution

Today, Nvidia stands as one of the most valuable technology companies in the world, and its rise can be traced directly to Jensen Huang's relentless execution-driven leadership.

For Jensen, success wasn't about having the best idea—it was about executing better, faster, and with more precision than anyone else. His unrelenting commitment to execution transformed Nvidia from a struggling startup to a world-changing technology giant.And for those who sought to follow in his footsteps, he had one simple lesson:

"Ideas are worthless without execution. Show me what you've built."

Chapter 6: Turning Failure into a Revolution

Jensen Huang had always believed that failure was a stepping stone to success. In fact, his entire philosophy at Nvidia revolved around the idea that excellence is the capacity to take pain—to endure setbacks, learn from them, and come back stronger. But in the mid-1990s, when Nvidia's first GPU prototype, the NV1, failed spectacularly, it was a moment that tested his resilience more than ever before.

The Rise and Fall of the NV1

In the early 1990s, Nvidia was still a young company struggling to carve out a space in the competitive semiconductor industry. Huang and his co-founders, Chris Malachowsky and Curtis Priem, had a vision: to create a groundbreaking graphics accelerator that would set them apart from the giants of the industry. The NV1 was their first attempt at revolutionizing computer graphics.

At its core, the NV1 was an ambitious product. Unlike other graphics cards of the time, which relied on traditional polygon-based rendering, the NV1 used quadratic texture mapping—a novel and technically advanced approach that Nvidia believed would be the future of 3D graphics. The company invested heavily in the technology, convinced that they were on the cusp of something revolutionary.

However, there was one major problem: the industry was moving in a different direction.

While Nvidia had bet on quadratic texture mapping, the rest of the gaming industry, including major developers and Microsoft, had begun standardizing on polygonal rendering with Direct3D. This meant that games designed for mainstream graphics cards were incompatible with the NV1.

When the NV1 launched in 1995, the response was underwhelming. Despite its impressive hardware capabilities, it failed to gain traction because very few developers supported its architecture. Most game studios had already optimized their titles for Direct3D, making it nearly impossible for the NV1 to compete.

For Nvidia, the NV1 wasn't just a disappointing product—it was an existential crisis. The company had poured vast amounts of resources into developing and marketing a technology that almost no one wanted. Investors were growing restless, competitors were surging ahead, and internally, Nvidia was facing the sobering realization that they had miscalculated the market's trajectory.

Rather than shifting blame, Jensen Huang did something unusual for a Silicon Valley CEO: he took full responsibility.

At a critical investor meeting following the NV1's failure, Huang stood before Nvidia's backers and admitted that they had made a mistake. He personally apologized for the misstep, acknowledging that the company had failed to anticipate where the industry was heading.

"We got it wrong," he told investors. "We bet on the wrong technology. But this is not the end of Nvidia. We will fix this."

His candidness was a stark contrast to the corporate culture of the time, where executives often deflected blame onto external factors or lower-level employees. But Huang understood something fundamental: trust was more important than pride. By openly admitting fault, he not only preserved Nvidia's credibility but also reinforced a crucial lesson within the company—it was okay to fail, as long as you learned from it.

The Birth of the GeForce 256

Huang knew that Nvidia's next move had to be decisive. The company couldn't afford another misstep. If Nvidia was going to survive, it needed to pivot—and fast.

Rather than dwelling on the NV1's failure, Huang redirected his team's focus toward understanding the needs of the market. He pushed Nvidia's engineers to study Direct3D, analyze what had gone wrong with the NV1, and develop a new product that aligned with industry standards while still showcasing Nvidia's technical prowess.

Over the next few years, Nvidia worked tirelessly to develop the world's first GPU, the GeForce 256. Unlike the NV1, the GeForce 256 was designed to be fully compatible with Direct3D, ensuring widespread support from game developers. More importantly, it introduced hardware transform and lighting (T&L), an innovation that dramatically improved rendering speeds and visual fidelity.

The GeForce 256 was not just another graphics card—it was a paradigm shift in computing. By offloading key graphics computations from the CPU to the GPU, it paved the way for modern graphics processing and, ultimately, the rise of AI-driven computing.

When the GeForce 256 launched in 1999, it changed everything. Reviewers hailed it as a groundbreaking achievement in computer graphics, game developers embraced its capabilities, and most importantly, it reaffirmed Nvidia's place in the industry.

The success of the GeForce 256 was the direct result of Huang's ability to turn failure into opportunity. Instead of allowing the NV1's failure to cripple Nvidia, he used it as motivation to build something better. His ability to acknowledge mistakes, pivot rapidly, and execute with precision became the cornerstone of The Nvidia Way—a relentless pursuit of innovation fueled by discipline and learning from setbacks.

Looking back, the NV1 was a failure—but an essential failure. Without it, Nvidia might never have recognized the importance of aligning with industry standards. Without Huang's public acknowledgment of the mistake, Nvidia might not have retained the trust of its investors. And without the painful lessons learned from NV1, the GeForce 256 might never have been born.

For Jensen Huang, the lesson was clear: great companies are not the ones that never fail. They are the ones that learn to fail intelligently.

Decades later, as Nvidia became a global leader in AI computing, the story of the NV1 remained an important chapter in its history. Engineers and executives alike would recall Huang's unwavering commitment to admitting failure, learning fast, and executing even faster.

As Huang himself would later say: "The pain of failure is temporary, but the lessons last forever. The only true failure is failing to learn."

The Art of Clarity

Jensen Huang never had much patience for wasted words. In an industry where ambiguity and technical jargon often clouded communication, he developed a reputation for being direct, almost brutally so. It wasn't an affectation or a quirk of personality—it was a survival mechanism, a leadership philosophy, and the cornerstone of what made Nvidia one of the most valuable technology companies in the world.

From the moment he founded Nvidia in 1993, Huang made it clear that he would tolerate no fluff, no hedging, and no excuses. His philosophy of direct and blunt communication wasn't just about cutting through corporate bureaucracy—it was about ensuring that everyone on his team understood exactly what needed to be done and had the clarity to execute it with precision.

Huang's communication style was shaped in part by his early experiences. Growing up as an immigrant child in the United States, he had to learn English quickly, not just for survival but for mastery. His mother made sure of it, drilling ten new words into his vocabulary every day. By the time he was a teenager, he spoke with the confidence of someone who had something to prove.

But it wasn't just linguistic fluency that shaped him—it was the understanding that words had weight. His early years in a tough Kentucky boarding school, where he had been mistakenly placed in a reform institution rather than the elite preparatory academy his parents had envisioned, reinforced the lesson that to be heard, he had to be direct. There was no room for ambiguity in a place where survival often depended on how clearly you could make your intentions known.

This ability to command attention through clarity followed him into his professional career. As he rose through the ranks at AMD and LSI Logic, it became evident that he had no tolerance for empty platitudes or vague directives. Colleagues noted that when Huang spoke, people listened—not because he was loud, but because he was precise. He had a knack for distilling complex ideas into their simplest, most actionable form.

Nvidia's First Lesson

When Nvidia was still in its infancy, Huang's style of communication became a defining aspect of the company culture. He knew that in the fast-moving world of technology, hesitation and miscommunication could kill a company before it even got off the ground. He made it clear from the start that Nvidia would be a place where ideas were debated fiercely, where the best ideas would win, and where every employee would be expected to express their thoughts with confidence and clarity.

Meetings at Nvidia were unlike those at most corporations. There were no long-winded PowerPoint presentations, no beating around the bush, no sugar-coating failures. Engineers were expected to come prepared with facts, data, and solutions. Huang set the tone by leading with questions that demanded precise answers. "What problem are we solving?" he would ask, often cutting off any response that meandered. If someone offered an answer that was vague or overly complicated, he would respond with his characteristic bluntness: "That doesn't make sense. Try again."

This kind of directness could be jarring for some, especially for those coming from more traditional corporate environments. But for those who adapted to

Huang's style, it became a superpower. They learned to communicate with the same efficiency and clarity that he demanded, and in doing so, they became better engineers, better problem-solvers, and better leaders themselves.

While Huang's communication style was unyielding, it was never mean-spirited. He didn't believe in humiliating employees or tearing people down just for the sake of it. Instead, his bluntness came from a place of respect—he believed that his employees were smart enough to handle the truth and that by being honest, he was giving them the opportunity to improve.

This honesty extended to himself as well. He was ruthless in his self-evaluation, often admitting his own mistakes before anyone else had the chance to point them out. He didn't see failure as something to be ashamed of—it was just another piece of data to analyze, another problem to solve. "I've made every mistake you can possibly make," he once said. "But the important thing is that we learn from them and never make the same mistake twice."

This culture of honest, unvarnished feedback became one of Nvidia's greatest strengths. Engineers weren't afraid to speak up in meetings. They weren't afraid to challenge ideas, even if those ideas came from Huang himself. He had made it clear from the start: Nvidia was not a place for people who wanted to play politics or tiptoe around difficult conversations. It was a place for people who wanted to do their best work, and that required absolute clarity.

The Whiteboard Doctrine

One of the most enduring symbols of Huang's leadership style was the whiteboard. While other CEOs preferred slide decks and reports, Huang preferred markers and an empty surface. Meetings at Nvidia often revolved around whiteboarding sessions where ideas were sketched out in real time, debated, and refined on the spot.

The whiteboard, in Huang's view, was the ultimate tool for clear thinking. It forced people to articulate their ideas concisely, to visualize their reasoning, and to make their thought process transparent. If you couldn't explain something clearly enough to put it on the whiteboard, then you probably didn't understand it well enough.

There was no hiding behind slides or corporate jargon in a whiteboarding session with Huang. He expected his team to think deeply, to communicate succinctly, and to be ready to defend their ideas. This method not only encouraged directness but also fostered a culture where the best ideas could be identified and acted upon quickly. It became a core part of how Nvidia operated—fast, focused, and always moving forward.

Huang's approach to communication extended beyond the walls of Nvidia. His direct style made him a formidable presence in industry conferences, board meetings, and investor calls. Unlike some executives who spoke in carefully hedged corporate-speak, Huang was known for his ability to deliver crisp, unambiguous insights. Whether he was explaining the future of AI, the power of GPUs, or Nvidia's latest technological breakthrough, he did so in a way that left no room for misunderstanding.

Investors appreciated it. Engineers respected it. And competitors feared it. Because when Jensen Huang spoke, there was no doubt about what he meant.

In the end, Huang's communication philosophy was about more than just being direct—it was about achieving clarity. He understood that in a world driven by complexity, clarity was a competitive advantage. It allowed Nvidia to move faster, to innovate more aggressively, and to avoid the pitfalls of indecision and misalignment.

For those who worked with him, it was a lesson that extended beyond the walls of Nvidia. Clarity, they learned, wasn't just about choosing the right words—it was about thinking clearly, acting decisively, and always being honest about what needed to be done.

Jensen Huang never wasted words. And in an industry where the right words at the right time could change everything, that made all the difference.

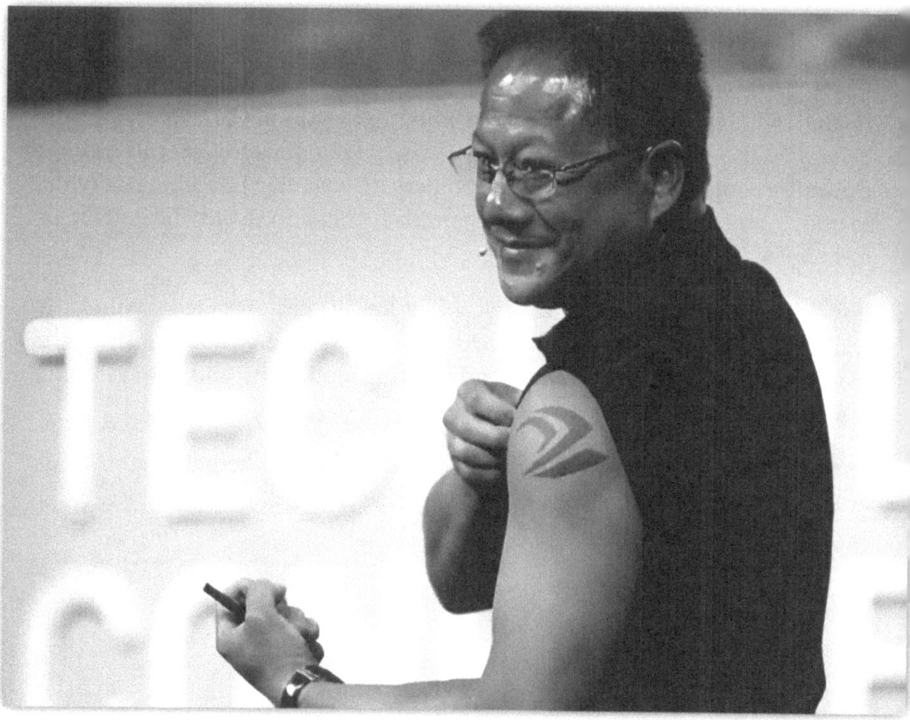

Chapter 7: The Relentless Critic

Jensen Huang's journey as a leader is not merely one of triumph but of unflinching self-examination. If there is one trait that sets him apart from the typical Silicon Valley CEO, it is his relentless self-criticism—a quality that has shaped Nvidia's culture, decision-making, and ultimately, its rise to dominance in the semiconductor industry.

From the very beginning of his career, Huang exhibited an almost brutal honesty when assessing his own performance. Unlike many leaders who externalize failures, he made it a habit to internalize them, to dissect every misstep with forensic precision. He often remarked that failure was the best teacher and that his ability to criticize himself more than anyone else allowed him to learn faster than his competitors.

Lessons in Pain

The origins of Huang's self-criticism can be traced back to his childhood and early career. Raised in a family that valued discipline and perseverance, he was taught that mistakes were inevitable, but learning from them was a choice. When his parents sent him and his brother to a reform school in Kentucky—mistaking it for a prestigious prep school—Huang did not allow himself to feel like a victim. Instead, he treated the hardship as a lesson in resilience. The relentless bullying, the isolation, the discomfort—it was all preparation for a world that rarely rewards weakness.

By the time Huang founded Nvidia in 1993, he had already endured his share of setbacks. But none were as painful as the company's first major failure: the NV1 graphics card. Conceived with a vision to revolutionize gaming, the NV1 was technologically ahead of its time but fundamentally misaligned with market needs. When it flopped, Nvidia was pushed to the brink of collapse. Huang did not blame the engineers, nor did he attribute the failure to external forces. Instead, he turned the scrutiny inward. He conducted exhaustive post-mortems, listing every mistake in painful detail.

"We overdesigned it," he admitted in later interviews. "We put in features nobody wanted. We thought we knew better than the market."

That admission marked a pivotal moment in his leadership style. Where other CEOs might have sought to protect their egos, Huang made it clear that self-deception was the enemy. If Nvidia was to survive, it would require a culture where mistakes were acknowledged immediately and corrected even faster.

One of the hallmarks of Huang's leadership is his insistence on brutal honesty, both with himself and his team. Unlike some leaders who surround themselves with yes-men, Huang encourages dissenting opinions. He often plays the role of his own harshest critic in meetings, forcing his executives to confront difficult truths. He has been known to walk into a room, look at a proposal, and bluntly declare, "This is garbage. Start over."

To some, this might sound demoralizing, but at Nvidia, it is a badge of honor. Employees know that Huang holds himself to an even higher standard. When Nvidia faced production delays in its early years, Huang did not blame supply chain issues or unforeseen obstacles. Instead, he berated himself for failing to anticipate problems.

"I should have seen this coming," he told his team. "I should have pushed harder."

This mindset created an environment where accountability was not just expected but revered. Employees quickly learned that mistakes were not to be hidden but exposed and addressed. Huang's philosophy was simple: the faster you recognize failure, the faster you can correct it.

The CEO Who Never Settles

Even at the peak of Nvidia's success, Huang has remained his own toughest critic. In 2011, when Nvidia launched the Tegra chip for mobile devices, expectations were high. The product performed well but failed to achieve the market dominance Huang had envisioned.

"I was too slow," he later admitted. "We hesitated. We let competitors catch up."

Rather than celebrate the moderate success, Huang fixated on the failure to dominate. He dissected every decision, every delay, every missed opportunity. His conclusion? Nvidia had to move faster, be more aggressive, and take bolder risks.

This self-criticism fueled a shift in the company's strategy. No longer would Nvidia merely compete—it would seek to define the future. This philosophy led to Nvidia's aggressive push into artificial intelligence, a move that transformed the company from a graphics card manufacturer into an AI powerhouse. Today, Nvidia's GPUs are at the heart of AI research, powering everything from deep learning to autonomous vehicles.

A Culture of Relentless Improvement

Huang's self-criticism is not just a personal trait; it has become the foundation of Nvidia's culture. At the company, failure is not a mark of shame but a step toward improvement. Engineers are encouraged to question their own assumptions, to find flaws before competitors do.

Huang himself sets the example. He does not shy away from admitting mistakes publicly. He once told a group of young engineers, "If you're not embarrassed by your last project, you're not learning fast enough."

This culture has led to a company that is constantly reinventing itself. Nvidia has pivoted multiple times in its history—from gaming to AI, from hardware to software—because it is never satisfied with the status quo. And that mindset stems from its founder.

The Legacy of a Relentless Critic

In the annals of business history, many great leaders have been known for their confidence, their vision, their ability to inspire. Jensen Huang possesses all of these traits, but what sets him apart is his willingness to be his own most unforgiving judge.

He once said, "Greatness is not intelligence. Greatness comes from character." And for Huang, character is forged through the fire of self-examination.

The reason Nvidia has remained at the cutting edge for decades is not just because it has brilliant engineers or groundbreaking technology. It is because its leader refuses to believe that success is permanent. Every product, every decision, every milestone is scrutinized, deconstructed, and improved upon.

As long as Jensen Huang is at the helm, Nvidia will never rest. Because its leader never stops looking in the mirror, never stops questioning, and never stops demanding more—from himself and from those around him.

That is the power of ruthless self-criticism. And that is the foundation of Nvidia's enduring success.

Chapter 8: Seeing the Future Before It Arrives

In the world of technology, even the biggest companies can find themselves on the brink of disaster. For NVIDIA, that moment came in the early 2000s when a series of unexpected setbacks pushed the company to the edge of financial ruin. Most CEOs in such a position might have looked for a quick exit—selling the company, slashing costs, or scaling back operations. But Jensen Huang, NVIDIA's co-founder and CEO, wasn't like most CEOs. Instead of retreating, he doubled down on innovation and made a series of bold decisions that not only saved the company but set it on a path to industry dominance.

The Crisis: A Lost Contract and Financial Disaster

At the start of the new millennium, NVIDIA was on a high. The company had grown rapidly throughout the late 1990s, capitalizing on the rise of 3D graphics in gaming. By 1999, it had gone public, and its GPUs were becoming the gold standard in PC gaming. But as the tech industry entered the early 2000s, a major crisis struck.

NVIDIA had been vying for a critical contract with a major console manufacturer. This deal, if secured, would have provided a steady stream of revenue and positioned NVIDIA as a dominant player in gaming beyond the PC market. But in a shocking turn of events, the company lost the contract to a competitor. The fallout was immediate. Investors panicked, stock prices plummeted, and internally, there was a sense of impending doom. NVIDIA's future had never looked more uncertain.

For many executives, the logical course of action in such a situation would have been to consider selling the company. With mounting financial losses and no clear path to recovery, selling to a larger tech firm could have provided an escape route. But Huang saw things differently. He believed in NVIDIA's potential and refused to let a single setback define its future.

Despite the growing pressure, Huang made it clear to his leadership team: selling NVIDIA was not an option. He was convinced that the company's best days were ahead, not behind. Instead of focusing on what had been lost, he turned his attention to what NVIDIA could still achieve.

Huang's decision to stay the course wasn't just about optimism—it was about strategy. He understood that while NVIDIA had suffered a setback, it still had world-class engineers, cutting-edge technology, and a growing base of loyal customers. The real question wasn't whether NVIDIA could survive, but how it could pivot and find new opportunities.

Determined to turn things around, Huang and his team aggressively pursued new business opportunities. One of those opportunities came in the form of Microsoft's upcoming gaming console, the Xbox. At the time, Microsoft was preparing to enter the console market, and it needed a powerful graphics processor that could compete with Sony's PlayStation.

Huang saw this as NVIDIA's chance for redemption. He personally led the negotiations with Microsoft, making the case that NVIDIA's GPUs were the best choice for the Xbox. It was a high-stakes move—the company was already struggling, and losing another major deal could have been catastrophic. But Huang's persistence paid off. After months of discussions, NVIDIA secured the contract to provide GPUs for the first-generation Xbox.

The deal was a game-changer. Not only did it provide the financial stability NVIDIA desperately needed, but it also positioned the company as a major player in the console gaming market. The Xbox partnership gave NVIDIA the momentum it needed to recover from its earlier setback and set the stage for even greater achievements.

With the Xbox contract secured, Huang didn't stop there. He recognized that NVIDIA couldn't rely on gaming alone to sustain its growth. The company needed to innovate and expand into new markets. Under his leadership, NVIDIA began investing heavily in research and development, exploring how GPUs could be used beyond gaming.

This period of reinvention led to some of NVIDIA's most significant breakthroughs. The company's advances in parallel computing paved the way for the development of CUDA, a revolutionary platform that allowed GPUs to be used for artificial intelligence, scientific research, and data processing. What had started as a crisis had now become a turning point, pushing NVIDIA to think bigger and redefine its role in the tech industry.

Fast forward two decades, and NVIDIA is no longer just a gaming company—it's a trillion-dollar AI powerhouse. Its GPUs power everything from deep learning and self-driving cars to medical research and cloud computing. The decision Huang made in the early 2000s—to hold on, to innovate, and to refuse to sell—set the foundation for NVIDIA's future success.

Looking back, it's clear that the crisis NVIDIA faced wasn't just a financial challenge—it was a test of leadership. Many companies would have folded under similar circumstances. But Huang's belief in his company, his willingness to take risks, and his relentless drive to push forward transformed what could have been NVIDIA's downfall into its greatest comeback story.

Today, NVIDIA is not only a leader in AI and gaming but a symbol of resilience and visionary leadership. And it all started with one crucial decision: to never give up.

Recognizing the Power of Parallelism

Jensen Huang had always possessed an uncanny ability to see the invisible—to anticipate shifts in technology before they became apparent to others. In the world of semiconductors and computing, where fortunes were made and lost on the margins of innovation, his foresight was not just a competitive advantage; it was a survival trait.

In the mid-1990s, the landscape of computing was shifting. Graphics processing units (GPUs) were still seen as specialized components, mostly useful for video games and niche applications. The central processing unit (CPU) reigned supreme, dictating the pace of software development and system architecture. Yet, Jensen saw something that few others did: the GPU was destined to do much more than render pixels on a screen. He envisioned a world where parallel processing, the fundamental nature of GPU architecture, could be harnessed for a broader range of computational tasks. It was a vision that would eventually lead to the explosion of artificial intelligence, deep learning, and the redefinition of computing itself.

Jensen's conviction about the power of GPUs wasn't based on a hunch. It was rooted in deep technical understanding. At a time when the industry was optimizing CPUs for faster sequential processing, he saw the limitations of that approach. While CPUs executed one task at a time with increasing speed, GPUs could process thousands of operations simultaneously.

The realization came not just from his engineering expertise, but from his willingness to challenge conventional wisdom. Nvidia, which he co-founded in 1993, initially focused on gaming and graphics acceleration. The company's first major breakthrough came with the GeForce 256 in 1999, which Nvidia called the "world's first GPU." This term wasn't just a marketing gimmick; it represented a fundamental shift in how graphics processing was conceived. But even as Nvidia dominated the gaming industry, Jensen was thinking far beyond entertainment.

By the early 2000s, computational scientists were starting to experiment with GPUs for tasks beyond graphics. The realization that GPUs could dramatically accelerate certain types of mathematical computations sparked Jensen's imagination. If properly harnessed, the power of parallel processing could revolutionize fields from medical research to scientific simulations. The challenge, however, was making this power accessible to non-specialists.

The Bet on CUDA

In 2006, Jensen made one of the most pivotal bets in Nvidia's history: the launch of CUDA (Compute Unified Device Architecture). At the time, the idea of using GPUs for general-purpose computing was still in its infancy. The industry had little appetite for such an approach, and many dismissed it as a distraction from Nvidia's core gaming business. But Jensen was undeterred.

He directed Nvidia's engineers to create an entirely new programming model that would allow developers to leverage the parallel computing capabilities of GPUs for tasks beyond graphics. It was a bold move, requiring not just technical innovation but also an effort to persuade an industry to rethink how computing was done.

For years, CUDA was largely ignored outside of niche scientific circles. But Jensen was patient. He understood that paradigm shifts take time. He also knew that, once developers saw the potential, adoption would accelerate. He invested heavily in making CUDA accessible, offering training programs, toolkits, and extensive support for researchers and developers willing to experiment.

Then, in the early 2010s, something extraordinary happened: the AI revolution began.

Artificial intelligence had long been a dream of computer scientists, but progress was slow. Traditional CPUs struggled to handle the massive amounts of data and computation required for deep learning models. That changed when researchers realized that Nvidia's GPUs, thanks to their parallel processing capabilities, were ideally suited for training neural networks.

Jensen's foresight had positioned Nvidia at the center of this transformation. By the time AI researchers like Geoffrey Hinton, Yann LeCun, and Yoshua Bengio were demonstrating the power of deep learning, Nvidia had already spent years refining CUDA and GPU acceleration. The research community turned to Nvidia's hardware, and demand skyrocketed.

When AlexNet, a deep learning model trained on Nvidia GPUs, won the 2012 ImageNet competition by a staggering margin, it marked the beginning of a new era. Suddenly, every major technology company—from Google to

Facebook to Microsoft—was investing heavily in AI. And at the heart of this revolution was Nvidia.

Jensen didn't just ride the wave; he accelerated it. He doubled down on AI, shifting Nvidia's strategy toward data centers, autonomous vehicles, and AI-driven applications. The company developed specialized hardware like the Tesla and later the Ampere and Hopper architectures, optimizing GPUs for machine learning workloads. Nvidia was no longer just a gaming company—it had become the backbone of AI infrastructure worldwide.

Even as Nvidia cemented its dominance in AI, Jensen was already looking ahead. He understood that the next frontier of computing would be driven by a convergence of AI, high-performance computing, and simulation. This led to the creation of the Nvidia Omniverse, a platform designed for building and simulating virtual worlds. The Omniverse wasn't just about gaming; it was about digital twins, industrial design, robotics, and the future of the metaverse.

Jensen saw that as AI models became more powerful, they would need simulated environments to train and operate. Autonomous vehicles, for example, required millions of miles of simulated driving before they could be deployed safely on real roads. The Omniverse provided a solution, allowing developers to create highly detailed, physics-accurate virtual worlds.

At the same time, he continued to push Nvidia into new domains: quantum computing, edge AI, and the intersection of biology and computing. Jensen understood that innovation is not about reacting to the present but anticipating the future. While others were still catching up to AI, he was already preparing for the next major shift.

Jensen Huang's success was never about chasing trends; it was about recognizing fundamental shifts before they became obvious. His ability to bet on long-term technological transformations—whether it was GPUs for general computing, AI acceleration, or the Omniverse—set Nvidia apart from its competitors.

But this vision wasn't just about intuition. It was built on rigorous technical understanding, relentless execution, and an unwavering belief in the power of computation. Jensen didn't wait for the market to tell him where to go; he built the future and then showed the world why it mattered.

As Nvidia continued to redefine computing, one thing remained certain: Jensen Huang would always be thinking several steps ahead, seeing the world not as it was, but as it could be.

Chapter 9: Swarming the Greatest Opportunity

Jensen Huang had always believed that success was not about chasing opportunities but about identifying and completely dominating the ones that mattered. It was a philosophy ingrained in him from the early days of Nvidia, a mindset that separated him from his competitors. When he saw an opening, he didn't hesitate; he mobilized his entire company like a general preparing for war. This wasn't just about seizing an opportunity—it was about swarming it with such force and precision that there would be no room left for anyone else.

The Power of Focus

Throughout his career, Jensen had observed that many companies failed not because they lacked intelligence or resources, but because they spread themselves too thin. They dabbled in multiple projects, hoping that at least one would pay off. This was not how he operated. If something was worth doing, it was worth committing to entirely.

One of the earliest examples of this approach came during Nvidia's pivot to graphics processing units (GPUs). When Nvidia was founded in 1993, the computing industry was largely focused on central processing units (CPUs). Companies like Intel and AMD dominated the landscape, and it would have been easy for a new company to try and compete in that space. But Jensen saw a different path. He recognized that the emerging world of computer graphics—driven by gaming and visual computing—needed specialized hardware. Instead of dividing Nvidia's efforts across multiple domains, he made a bold bet: Nvidia would become the leader in GPUs, even if it meant turning down other lucrative opportunities.

This decision wasn't made lightly. The company had already suffered setbacks with its early products. Nvidia's first graphics card, the NV1, had been a commercial failure. Many executives in his position would have opted for a more diversified strategy to hedge their bets. But Jensen did the opposite. He doubled down. Rather than abandoning the GPU market, he refined Nvidia's approach and made the company synonymous with high-performance graphics. The result was the RIVA 128 in 1997, which was a massive success and set Nvidia on its trajectory toward dominance.

Jensen's ability to see potential where others didn't was one of his greatest strengths. It wasn't just about being innovative—it was about recognizing that the biggest opportunities often seemed insignificant at first. The best example of this came in the early 2000s when he realized that GPUs could be used for far more than just gaming.

Most people, even within Nvidia, saw the GPU as a tool for rendering graphics. But Jensen saw something else: raw computational power. He knew that GPUs had massively parallel architectures that could handle complex calculations much more efficiently than CPUs. While most of the industry was still focused on traditional computing models, he saw an opening in scientific computing, artificial intelligence, and deep learning.

Again, he didn't hesitate. Instead of treating GPU computing as a side project, he turned it into a central mission for Nvidia. He aggressively invested in CUDA (Compute Unified Device Architecture), a programming model that allowed developers to use Nvidia's GPUs for general-purpose computing. This move was initially met with skepticism. Many believed it was a distraction, a niche market at best. But Jensen understood the long-term potential. He swarmed the opportunity, pouring resources into it until it became impossible for competitors to catch up.

All In

By the mid-2010s, Jensen's strategy of swarming opportunities reached its most dramatic phase. The rise of artificial intelligence had created a seismic shift in computing, and once again, Nvidia was positioned to take advantage. Deep learning was transforming industries, from healthcare to autonomous driving, but the real breakthrough came when AI researchers realized that GPUs were the key to training neural networks at unprecedented speeds.

Jensen didn't just recognize this trend—he ensured that Nvidia owned it. He didn't merely invest in AI; he made it the company's core identity. Nvidia shifted its focus from being a gaming company to becoming an AI powerhouse. The company poured billions into research and development, hiring the best AI scientists, building AI-specific hardware like the Tesla V100, and forming strategic partnerships with leading AI labs.

While other companies hesitated, Nvidia moved at lightning speed. The result? By the time competitors began to take AI seriously, Nvidia had already established an unshakable lead. Today, Nvidia's GPUs are the backbone of AI research, used by every major AI company, from Google to OpenAI.

One of the key reasons Jensen's approach worked so well was his execution. Swarming an opportunity wasn't just about investing money or making bold statements—it was about flawless execution at every level. This meant creating an internal culture where everyone understood the mission and worked with relentless urgency.

Jensen was known for his extreme focus on detail. He didn't delegate major strategic decisions—he was directly involved in product roadmaps, hiring, and even marketing strategies. His hands-on leadership ensured that Nvidia didn't just enter markets; it dominated them.

For example, when Nvidia entered the autonomous vehicle space, it didn't do so half-heartedly. The company built DRIVE, a complete AI platform for self-driving cars. It wasn't just hardware—it was a full-stack solution that included software, data processing, and simulation tools. By offering a comprehensive ecosystem, Nvidia made itself indispensable to the automotive industry. Tesla, Mercedes, and many others built their autonomous driving technologies on Nvidia's platform.

Jensen Huang's ability to swarm the greatest opportunities is what turned Nvidia from a small startup into a trillion-dollar company. It wasn't about luck or being in the right place at the right time—it was about decisiveness, conviction, and the ability to execute at scale.

His philosophy of total commitment to a singular vision is a lesson for any entrepreneur. Opportunities are everywhere, but success belongs to those who recognize them early and move so aggressively that they leave no room for competition.

Looking at Nvidia's future, one thing remains certain: whenever the next great technological revolution emerges, Jensen will be the first to see it. And when he does, he won't just participate—he will swarm it, ensuring that Nvidia remains the dominant force in whatever comes next.

The Art of Precision

Jensen Huang had always believed that details were not mere finishing touches; they were the foundation upon which success was built. His leadership at Nvidia was not simply about vision or technological breakthroughs—it was about an unrelenting focus on getting everything right, down to the finest element. Whether it was the architecture of a new GPU, the structure of an earnings call, or the way Nvidia's logo appeared on a conference backdrop, Huang scrutinized every component with the sharp eye of a craftsman. In an era where leaders often delegated the details, he immersed himself in them.

This was no accident. It was the product of a lifetime of learning, a trait embedded in him from his early days. From an immigrant child in Kentucky, navigating an unfamiliar language and culture, to a graduate student balancing family life and a job at AMD, Jensen's ability to fixate on details with surgical precision had been a source of survival. And later, at Nvidia, it became a key reason why his company would lead the world in AI computing.

The culture of Nvidia was shaped by Huang's meticulousness. The company's employees learned early that their CEO had a photographic memory, an uncanny ability to recall details about products, competitors, and past conversations with employees. At times, his insistence on perfection made meetings tense. A slipshod explanation or an unpolished presentation could mean a redo, no matter the employee's seniority. If Huang could spot a single inconsistency in an internal review, he would pause and challenge his team, asking, "Is this really the best we can do?"

He was famous for the way he handled product launches. Engineers knew that Jensen expected them to sweat the smallest aspects—heat dissipation, power efficiency, memory bandwidth. The Nvidia RTX 3090, a card that pushed the limits of real-time ray tracing, was a testament to that philosophy. It wasn't enough that it was fast; Huang wanted it optimized in ways that no competitor had even considered. Nvidia's competitors designed for performance; Nvidia, under Huang, designed for endurance, efficiency, and future-proofing.

His obsession extended beyond hardware. Software, often an afterthought for chip companies, was equally important. When launching CUDA, Nvidia's parallel computing platform, Huang personally reviewed presentations, simplified explanations, and ensured the branding communicated the immense shift it represented. He demanded a level of refinement that others might have dismissed as excessive. But in his mind, if an idea was revolutionary, it had to be presented in the clearest, most compelling way.

Inside the Boardroom: A Relentless Pursuit of Excellence

Jensen's scrutiny wasn't limited to product development. When it came to business decisions, he was just as particular. Before earnings calls, he reviewed every detail of the financial reports, questioning figures and scrutinizing projections. Nvidia's investor relations team quickly realized that nothing could be left unchecked—Huang would remember specific numbers from previous quarters, challenge inconsistencies, and refuse to allow vague answers to pass.

This precision was also apparent in Nvidia's acquisition strategies. When acquiring Mellanox, a deal that would bolster Nvidia's data center business, Huang was deeply involved in the negotiation process. Rather than leaving it to a team of lawyers and strategists, he read through contracts, assessed the synergy between the two companies at an operational level, and even reviewed customer feedback on Mellanox's existing products. The decision to pursue the acquisition was not just about financial viability; it was about ensuring that every aspect of the integration aligned with Nvidia's long-term objectives.

Public Speaking: A CEO Who Leaves Nothing to Chance

Huang's attention to detail extended into his public appearances. Unlike many executives who relied heavily on speechwriters, he was known to personally refine his keynote presentations. When unveiling a new GPU or AI breakthrough, every word, slide, and transition was carefully considered. His team knew that he would practice late into the night, rehearsing not just what he would say, but how he would say it—his tone, his pauses, his gestures.

A defining moment of his precision in public speaking came during Nvidia's push into artificial intelligence. In a keynote where he introduced the DGX-1, Nvidia's first AI supercomputer, Huang didn't just talk about the hardware. He told a story. He described how AI would change the world, how deep learning was already transforming industries, and how Nvidia had built the technology to accelerate that transformation. The seamlessness of his presentation was not accidental; it was the product of an exacting mind that left no room for imperfection.

A Workplace Culture Built on Precision

At Nvidia, this relentless focus on detail set the standard for the entire company. Employees quickly learned that "good enough" was not part of the company's vocabulary. A product that was 90% complete was still incomplete. Engineers were encouraged to iterate beyond their own expectations, to test for failure modes that might seem statistically improbable but could have catastrophic consequences if ignored.

Even the design of Nvidia's headquarters in Santa Clara reflected Huang's precision. The building, a striking geometric structure, was meant to encourage collaboration and cross-functional communication. Jensen personally reviewed elements of the design to ensure it reflected the culture of the company—open, interconnected, and forward-thinking.

Challenges of Perfectionism

While Huang's attention to detail had undoubtedly propelled Nvidia to the forefront of the tech industry, it also came with its challenges. Some executives found it exhausting to meet his exacting standards. A few had left the company, citing the relentless pace and pressure.

However, those who thrived under his leadership understood that his high standards weren't about control for its own sake—they were about ensuring that Nvidia remained ahead. "Jensen doesn't expect anything from us that he wouldn't expect from himself," an engineer once remarked. "And that's why we follow him."

Conclusion: The Legacy of a Detail-Oriented Visionary

Jensen Huang's meticulous approach has not only built one of the most formidable technology companies in the world but also cultivated a culture where excellence is a requirement, not an aspiration. His belief that details determine destiny has shaped Nvidia's trajectory from a scrappy startup to a global powerhouse.

In the end, his obsession with precision is not just about technology or business—it is about a philosophy of life. In a world that often celebrates shortcuts and speed, Huang remains a rare breed of leader who understands that true innovation lies in the details. And for Nvidia, that philosophy has made all the difference.

Chapter 10: The CEO Who Writes Back

In the fast-paced world of technology, where CEOs are often inaccessible figures hidden behind layers of executives and public relations teams, Jensen Huang stands apart. The co-founder and CEO of NVIDIA, a company that has revolutionized graphics processing and artificial intelligence, does something most tech leaders wouldn't even consider: he personally engages with fans, engineers, and AI researchers, often responding to their messages, acknowledging their work, and even sending unexpected gifts.

For many in the developer and AI community, the idea of a tech billionaire personally replying to emails or social media messages seems almost impossible. Yet, Huang has built a reputation for doing just that. Whether it's a university student experimenting with AI models or an independent developer building a breakthrough application on NVIDIA hardware, Huang has been known to send personal responses, offering encouragement, insights, or even invitations to discuss ideas further.

One particularly well-known instance of Huang's personal engagement happened when an AI researcher posted about their groundbreaking work using NVIDIA GPUs. The researcher had expected, at most, a few comments from fellow engineers. Instead, he received a direct message from Huang himself, congratulating him on his innovation and suggesting ways he could further optimize his model using NVIDIA's latest software stack. The researcher later described the experience as "a moment of validation I never expected in my career."

Huang doesn't just respond with words—he often backs his encouragement with action. NVIDIA fans who have contributed significantly to AI research or the gaming community have, on occasion, received surprise packages from the company. Some of these gifts include limited-edition GPUs, NVIDIA swag, and in some rare cases, personal handwritten notes from Huang. For tech enthusiasts and engineers, receiving a note or a package from the CEO himself feels like a once-in-a-lifetime event.

One such story involved a software developer who had spent months optimizing an open-source AI application that ran on NVIDIA hardware. The project gained traction in the developer community, and before long, it caught Huang's attention. Instead of simply acknowledging the achievement online, Huang went a step further—he sent the developer a state-of-the-art NVIDIA GPU along with a letter thanking him for his contributions to the AI ecosystem. The developer shared the experience on social media, calling it "the best email thread of my life."

Huang's approach to engaging with his fans and the developer community is not just a goodwill gesture—it's a strategic move that strengthens NVIDIA's bond with the people who use and shape its technology. By directly engaging with researchers and engineers, Huang ensures that NVIDIA remains not just a tech company but a community-driven innovation hub. His leadership style fosters loyalty and motivation among those who build on NVIDIA's platforms, creating a feedback loop of creativity and advancement.

Unlike traditional corporate communications, which are often filtered through public relations departments, Huang's messages feel personal and authentic. He doesn't reply with generic statements; he provides real insights, offers technical guidance, and sometimes even cracks jokes. Developers who have interacted with him often note how approachable he is, describing his enthusiasm for AI and graphics computing as contagious.

This culture of direct engagement has also influenced NVIDIA's corporate ethos. Many employees, inspired by Huang's example, actively participate in online forums, developer communities, and AI research groups, helping others optimize their work on NVIDIA hardware. It's a reflection of the company's philosophy: innovation thrives when ideas are shared, nurtured, and recognized.

Beyond emails and messages, Huang occasionally surprises fans at industry events. Attendees at AI conferences and gaming expos have recounted stories of Huang casually walking up to developers at NVIDIA booths, engaging them in deep technical discussions, and thanking them for their contributions. It's a stark contrast to the usual image of a corporate CEO who is only visible during keynote presentations.

One particularly memorable instance occurred at a gaming convention when a young programmer demoed a real-time rendering application running on an NVIDIA GPU. Huang, without introduction, joined the audience, watched for several minutes, and then walked up to the programmer to ask about the technical challenges he faced. After an in-depth discussion, he handed the developer his business card and told him to reach out if he ever needed help optimizing performance. The moment quickly went viral, further cementing Huang's reputation as a leader who truly values innovation at every level.

As NVIDIA continues to dominate the AI and gaming landscapes, Huang's hands-on approach to leadership remains one of the company's defining characteristics. In an age where automation and impersonal corporate culture are becoming the norm, his willingness to personally connect with fans and developers sets him—and NVIDIA—apart.

For those who have received a reply from him, it's more than just a message from a CEO; it's a moment of recognition that fuels their passion and ambition. It's proof that in a world of algorithms and machine learning, human connection still matters.

And that, perhaps, is Jensen Huang's greatest gift to the NVIDIA community.

The Day Jensen Huang Stole the Show

Harvard Business School is no stranger to guest speakers and unexpected moments of brilliance, but few could have predicted the electrifying lesson that unfolded when Jensen Huang, the co-founder and CEO of NVIDIA, unexpectedly took center stage. What began as a routine classroom discussion turned into an impromptu masterclass on corporate reinvention, leaving students and faculty in awe.

It was an ordinary afternoon in a business strategy class at Harvard. The discussion centered around the concept of corporate pivots—how companies evolve and shift strategies in response to changing markets. The professor posed a question to the class: "Can anyone name a company that has successfully pivoted its business model?" The students murmured, considering answers. Before the professor could respond, a voice from the back of the room cut through the silence.

"I can answer that."

The class turned to see a man standing up. Dressed in his signature black leather jacket, he exuded quiet confidence. At first, some students didn't recognize him, but as soon as he spoke again, it became clear: this was Jensen Huang, the legendary CEO of NVIDIA.

The professor, taken aback but intrigued, invited Huang to elaborate. The students leaned forward in anticipation, sensing that they were about to receive insights from a business leader who had transformed an entire industry.

Huang began by taking the class back to NVIDIA's early days. "When we started NVIDIA in 1993, our focus was on gaming graphics. We built GPUs that enhanced the visual experience for gamers, and for a long time, that was our core business. We were known as a gaming company, and we were really good at it. But being great at one thing doesn't guarantee survival forever. Markets change. Technology changes. And as leaders, we have to see beyond what we are today to what we could become."

The room was silent, absorbing his every word. Huang continued, explaining how NVIDIA, despite its dominance in gaming, realized that the underlying architecture of GPUs had far greater potential. "Around 2006, we made a bet that GPUs could do more than render graphics—they could power artificial intelligence. But at that time, no one was talking about AI the way they do now. The idea that GPUs could accelerate AI workloads wasn't mainstream yet."

He then detailed the pivotal decision that would change NVIDIA's future forever. "We invested heavily in CUDA, a parallel computing platform that allowed developers to program GPUs for tasks beyond gaming. It was a huge risk. Investors were skeptical. People thought we were crazy to spend so much time and money on something that didn't have an immediate market. But we saw the potential. We knew AI researchers needed faster computing power. So we built the tools they needed—before they even knew they needed them."

As Huang spoke, students began jotting down notes furiously. He wasn't just telling a story—he was teaching them a lesson in vision, risk-taking, and execution.

"Fast forward to today," he continued, "and AI has become one of the most important technological shifts in history. And guess what? Every major AI breakthrough—from deep learning to self-driving cars to ChatGPT—runs on NVIDIA GPUs. We didn't just pivot; we positioned ourselves at the center of an industry that barely existed when we started investing in it. That's how you reinvent a company."

One student raised a hand. "How did you know it would work?"Huang smiled. "We didn't. But great companies don't wait for certainty. If you wait until something is obvious, you're already too late. We had conviction. We listened to researchers. We saw small successes in the academic world before the commercial world caught on. And we doubled down. That's how you pivot—not by guessing, but by identifying trends before they become mainstream and having the courage to act on them."

The energy in the room was palpable. The professor, who had planned to give his own examples, instead let Huang continue. The CEO spoke about the importance of company culture in transformation. "A pivot isn't just about technology. It's about mindset. At NVIDIA, we hire people who are curious, who aren't afraid to question what's possible. That's what allowed us to make this leap. If you build a culture of relentless innovation, pivots become part of your DNA."

After speaking for nearly twenty minutes, Huang finally sat down. The room erupted in applause. The professor, still visibly impressed, turned back to the students. "Well, I think we've just had one of the best lectures of the semester."

The story of Jensen Huang's impromptu Harvard lecture quickly spread beyond the classroom. Students who had been there described it as a once-in-a-lifetime moment—a rare opportunity to hear, firsthand, how a CEO at the top of his game thinks about business transformation. The lesson went beyond NVIDIA; it was about the nature of innovation itself.

For Huang, it was just another day. He hadn't come to Harvard to teach a class, but when given the opportunity, he seized the moment. He demonstrated exactly what had made NVIDIA successful: the ability to recognize when to take the lead, when to speak up, and when to act decisively before anyone else does.As the students left the classroom, many knew they had just witnessed something special. One future entrepreneur turned to another and said, "I think we just saw a masterclass in leadership."

Indeed, they had.

The Relentless Drive of Jensen Huang

By the time he co-founded Nvidia in 1993, he had already learned one of the most valuable lessons in leadership: complacency is the enemy of innovation. Nvidia's early years were marked by struggle. The company's first product, the NV1, was a disaster. It was over-designed, bloated with features no one needed, and ultimately a commercial failure. For many founders, such a catastrophic misstep might have led to retreat. Not for Jensen. He viewed failure as an opportunity to sharpen his focus.

From the NV1 debacle, he extracted a critical lesson: "We learned it was better to do fewer things well than to do too many things poorly." Nvidia recalibrated, focusing on delivering the best possible graphics performance rather than trying to be everything at once. That shift in mindset set the company on a new trajectory.

Still, even when Nvidia began to find success, Jensen refused to let his company settle. He had seen what happened to companies that became comfortable. They fell behind. They got disrupted. "The moment you stop moving forward, you start dying," he once said.

As the world changed, so did Nvidia. Under Jensen's leadership, the company pivoted repeatedly, embracing artificial intelligence and deep learning at a time when most companies were still hesitant. In the early 2000s, Nvidia was primarily known for making graphics cards for gaming. That alone would have been a lucrative niche, but Jensen saw beyond the immediate horizon. He anticipated that GPUs could be used for far more than just rendering images on a screen. They could power artificial intelligence, accelerate scientific research, and revolutionize computing.

While competitors focused on incremental improvements, Nvidia invested heavily in AI. It was a gamble that could have backfired, but Jensen had no interest in playing it safe. "We were 10 years too early," he later admitted. "But better too early than too late." That decision ultimately positioned Nvidia at the forefront of the AI revolution, making it one of the most valuable technology companies in the world.

Even as Nvidia reached new heights, Jensen's mindset did not change. He did not dwell on past successes, nor did he allow them to slow him down. Each technological breakthrough was merely a stepping stone to the next challenge. "Complacency is what kills great companies," he often reminded his team. "We can never fall into that trap."

His leadership style reflected this philosophy. He was known for his intensity, his demand for excellence, and his refusal to accept mediocrity. At Nvidia, Jensen implemented a flat organizational structure—60 direct reports, no middle managers. He did not waste time with bureaucracy. He believed in speed, agility, and relentless iteration. He encouraged internal debate, viewing disagreement as a way to refine ideas. "Hone the sword through conflict," he would say.

Jensen also cultivated a culture where learning never stopped. He once told an interviewer, "If you're the same person you were five years ago, you're already obsolete." At Nvidia, employees were expected to evolve, to keep pushing themselves, to never settle for "good enough."

This philosophy extended to Jensen himself. Despite leading a multibillion-dollar company, he remained deeply involved in technology, constantly learning and adapting. He would personally whiteboard ideas with engineers, challenging them to think bigger and move faster.

For Jensen Huang, movement is not just a strategy—it is a way of life. The moment he stops moving forward is the moment he ceases to be the leader that built Nvidia into what it is today. Whether navigating personal hardships, pushing through professional setbacks, or pioneering new industries, his story is one of relentless drive, an unyielding commitment to progress.

As Nvidia continues to shape the future of computing, one thing remains certain: Jensen Huang will never be satisfied with where things are. There will always be a new challenge, a new frontier, a new opportunity to seize. Because for him, the only real failure is standing still.

Chapter 11: The Weight of Responsibility

In the high-stakes world of technology, where fortunes rise and fall with every market shift, leadership is often tested in times of crisis. Many CEOs rely on external factors to justify setbacks—market conditions, economic downturns, shifting consumer trends. But Jensen Huang, the co-founder and CEO of NVIDIA, stands apart. He embraces a leadership philosophy known as "Extreme Ownership," a concept that dictates total accountability, no excuses. When things go wrong, he doesn't point fingers—he takes responsibility. And in 2019, he proved just how powerful that mindset could be.

That year, NVIDIA faced one of its most challenging periods. After years of sustained growth, the company was hit with an unexpected downturn. The gaming market, a major driver of NVIDIA's revenue, slowed significantly. Data center sales, another growing sector for the company, didn't meet expectations. To make matters worse, the cryptocurrency boom that had fueled demand for GPUs suddenly collapsed, leaving a surplus of inventory. The result was a disastrous quarter that sent NVIDIA's stock price tumbling by nearly 50%.

For many executives, such a sharp decline would have been an opportunity to shift blame. Some might have pointed to unpredictable market conditions, changes in consumer demand, or even the broader economic landscape. But not Huang. Instead, he stood before investors, employees, and the media and took full responsibility.

"This is on me," he said during a company-wide meeting. "We made miscalculations. We should have anticipated the slowdown better. That's my failure, and I own it. But we are going to fix it, and we are going to come back stronger."

It was a defining moment for NVIDIA and a testament to Huang's leadership. His words weren't just empty reassurances—they were a rallying cry. Employees who might have otherwise felt discouraged instead felt motivated. Investors, despite their initial concerns, saw a leader who was willing to take ownership of mistakes rather than making excuses.

Huang wasted no time in leading the turnaround. Instead of retreating or making drastic cuts, he doubled down on innovation. He reassessed NVIDIA's long-term strategy, focusing on artificial intelligence, cloud computing, and autonomous vehicles—three sectors he believed would drive the future of technology. He encouraged his teams to think bigger, to take risks, and to push beyond the company's traditional markets.

One of the first major moves following the crisis was a renewed investment in AI. While NVIDIA had already been a leader in AI-driven computing, Huang recognized that the technology was evolving faster than many expected. He directed the company to accelerate development in deep learning and AI training frameworks, ensuring that NVIDIA's GPUs would remain at the forefront of artificial intelligence research.

At the same time, he took a strategic approach to addressing inventory issues. Rather than flooding the market with unsold GPUs at discounted rates—an approach that could have devalued NVIDIA's brand—Huang and his team worked on refining production cycles to align better with market demand. It was a calculated move that stabilized revenue streams without compromising the company's long-term vision.

Huang also reinforced the importance of company culture in overcoming adversity. He encouraged transparency, ensuring that every team understood the challenges at hand and the collective effort required to move forward. Employees were not kept in the dark about the financial struggles—rather, they were empowered with the knowledge that their contributions could help turn the situation around.

The results spoke for themselves. Within a year, NVIDIA not only recovered but reached new heights. By the end of 2020, the company's stock had soared to record levels, and its market value had surpassed $300 billion. AI became a core pillar of NVIDIA's business, with its GPUs powering breakthroughs in everything from natural language processing to healthcare research. The data center segment, once a struggling division, turned into a massive growth driver. The same company that had been doubted in 2019 was now leading the charge into the future of computing.

For Huang, the lessons of that difficult period reinforced his belief in Extreme Ownership. "When you take full responsibility, you gain control over the outcome," he later reflected. "If you blame the market or external conditions, you're giving away your power. But when you own the problem, you also own the solution."

Extreme Ownership

His approach to leadership has since become a defining feature of NVIDIA's culture. Employees at all levels are encouraged to take ownership of their work, to recognize their impact, and to be accountable for both successes and failures. It's a mindset that fosters resilience, agility, and, most importantly, long-term success.

Jensen Huang's embrace of Extreme Ownership is more than just a management philosophy—it's a testament to the power of accountability in building a world-class company. By refusing to make excuses and taking direct responsibility for NVIDIA's challenges, he not only saved the company from a crisis but also positioned it as a dominant force in AI, gaming, and cloud computing. His story is proof that true leadership isn't about avoiding failure—it's about how you respond when failure happens.

Jensen Huang has always believed that greatness is not measured solely by intelligence, but by character. And character, in his view, is forged through relentless accountability. In every phase of his life—whether as an immigrant child learning English word by word, a struggling entrepreneur facing near failure, or the CEO of Nvidia leading a trillion-dollar company—he has never once shirked responsibility. Extreme accountability, both in his leadership and personal standards, defines his approach to business and life.

Huang's deep sense of accountability was first instilled in him as a child. Born in Taiwan and later sent to the United States for better opportunities, he quickly learned that success would not come easy. His parents had sacrificed everything—selling their possessions to afford his and his brother's education, sending them ahead to America before they could make the journey themselves. Jensen internalized the weight of their sacrifice. He understood that he could not fail, that his success was not just his own but something owed to his family.

This early lesson in responsibility set the foundation for how he would later lead Nvidia. At the core of his leadership is the belief that to achieve anything meaningful, one must first hold oneself accountable to the highest possible standards.

Many CEOs delegate authority, distancing themselves from the consequences of poor decisions. Jensen Huang takes the opposite approach. He is known for being involved in every critical aspect of Nvidia's operations, from product development to hiring decisions. If something goes wrong, he does not shift blame—he owns it entirely.

In the early years of Nvidia, when the company was struggling, Huang had to lay off a significant portion of his workforce. It was an excruciating decision, and one he did not take lightly. But instead of placing the blame on external forces, poor market conditions, or bad luck, he shouldered the burden himself. He called a company-wide meeting and stood before his employees to tell them the harsh truth: the company had failed them. There were no excuses, no platitudes—only a vow to correct course and ensure that such mistakes were never repeated.

His belief in extreme accountability is perhaps best illustrated in his infamous statement: "If we fail, I won't blame the economy, I won't blame the competition, I won't blame the government. I will blame me." This mindset permeates every level of Nvidia. Employees know that when Jensen speaks, he means it. There is no hiding, no passing the buck—only facing the consequences and finding solutions.

A Culture of High Expectations

Huang's extreme accountability does not stop at himself. He demands the same from his team. At Nvidia, employees are expected to take full ownership of their projects, no matter how complex or difficult. There are no excessive layers of management to buffer individuals from responsibility. If you work at Nvidia, you are expected to deliver.

He is famous for calling out inefficiencies in real time, often in front of the entire team. To some, this might seem harsh, but to those who understand his leadership, it is simply the culture of excellence he has built. The expectation is clear: if you make a mistake, you own it. But that accountability comes with immense rewards. Employees who rise to the challenge gain Huang's trust, and with it, the autonomy to innovate and push boundaries.

His meetings are a testament to this philosophy. There are no lengthy, bureaucratic reports. Instead, discussions happen in real-time, usually at the whiteboard, where ideas are challenged and dissected on the spot. If someone presents a flawed plan, they must defend it immediately. If an engineer's design has flaws, they must address them now. Huang does not allow room for ambiguity—everyone must be accountable for their ideas, their work, and ultimately, the company's success.

Extreme accountability is not easy. It comes with stress, pressure, and a burden that most people would rather avoid. But Huang embraces it. He has often spoken about how leadership is about making the hard choices that no one else wants to make.

In Nvidia's early days, when the company was burning through cash and struggling to find its footing, many suggested he step down as CEO and let a more experienced executive take over. Instead, he doubled down. He took personal responsibility for every misstep, analyzing what had gone wrong and adjusting Nvidia's strategy accordingly. This willingness to take on responsibility, even when the stakes were at their highest, is what kept Nvidia alive when other startups faltered.

But extreme accountability also means taking responsibility even for the things you cannot control. When the 2008 financial crisis hit, many companies scrambled to cut costs and lay off employees. Nvidia was not immune to the downturn, but Huang refused to see it as an excuse. He told his team that while the crisis was beyond their control, their response to it was not. Instead of waiting for the market to recover, he pushed Nvidia to innovate, to develop new technologies that would put them ahead when the economy rebounded. That decision paid off in the long run, positioning Nvidia as a leader in graphics processing and AI computing.The key to Jensen Huang's success is that he does not see accountability as a burden, but as a privilege. He believes that to lead is to bear the weight of the vision and to ensure that it is realized, no matter what obstacles arise.

In 2016, when Nvidia made the bold pivot toward AI computing, many doubted whether the company could succeed. The industry was still skeptical about the true potential of AI, and competitors were hesitant to make similar bets. But Huang took full responsibility for the decision. He staked Nvidia's future on it, investing billions into research and development. If it had failed, it would have been his failure. But because he took full ownership of the risk, he was also able to steer Nvidia with conviction. Today, that decision has made Nvidia one of the most valuable technology companies in the world.

For Huang, accountability is not just about answering for mistakes—it is about being willing to take the bold steps necessary for greatness. His leadership is not reactive, but proactive. He does not wait for problems to arise; he anticipates them. He does not shy away from challenges; he welcomes them. And above all, he never leaves the fate of Nvidia in anyone's hands but his own.

Jensen Huang's approach to leadership has left an indelible mark on Nvidia and the tech industry at large. His philosophy of extreme accountability has created a company culture where excellence is not optional, where employees take ownership of their work, and where the pursuit of innovation is relentless.

As Nvidia continues to push the boundaries of AI, gaming, and high-performance computing, Huang remains at the helm, holding himself to the same high standards he always has. He knows that with great power comes great responsibility. And he welcomes it.Perhaps the greatest lesson from Jensen Huang's story is this: success is not about avoiding failure, but about taking full responsibility for every decision, every mistake, and every outcome. In his world, there are no excuses—only the relentless pursuit of greatness.

And that, above all, is what makes him one of the most extraordinary leaders of our time.

The Day Jensen Huang Fired Himself

Leadership is often defined by pivotal moments—decisions that shape the course of a company and redefine its future. For Jensen Huang, one such moment came when he made a radical, unconventional move: he fired himself.

At the time, NVIDIA was struggling. The company had carved out a niche in the graphics industry, but it was facing growing challenges. The market was shifting, and competitors were threatening its position. Its approach to growth, which had once seemed like the right strategy, was now faltering. Sales were lagging, product development cycles were misaligned with industry trends, and internal confidence was beginning to wane. Something had to change.

Huang, known for his relentless pursuit of innovation and his deep sense of responsibility, realized that the problem wasn't just the market. It wasn't just the competition. It wasn't even just the product lineup. The issue, he concluded, was leadership—his leadership. His approach, his mindset, and his strategic vision had reached a point where they were no longer delivering the results NVIDIA needed. And instead of blaming external factors or his executive team, he did something no one expected.

During an internal meeting with his leadership team, he stood up, looked around the room, and said, "Jensen Huang, the CEO who has led this company until today, is fired. He is no longer the right person to take NVIDIA where it needs to go. Starting now, a new Jensen Huang is taking over. And he's going to do things differently."

There was a stunned silence in the room. His executives exchanged glances, unsure of what to make of this declaration. Was this a symbolic gesture? Was he actually stepping down?

Huang clarified: "I am not stepping down. But the way I have been running this company is no longer good enough. I need to evolve, and so does NVIDIA. The old me is gone. The new me is taking charge, and we are going to rethink everything—our strategy, our execution, our products, and most importantly, our mindset."

It was a moment of radical self-accountability, unlike anything his team had seen before. CEOs rarely admit they need to change. Many cling to their previous decisions, defending past failures as misfortunes rather than mistakes. But Huang had no interest in preserving his ego—his only focus was making NVIDIA great.

That day marked a turning point. Huang led his team through an exhaustive reassessment of their business model. They scrutinized past decisions, analyzed market shifts, and debated what NVIDIA needed to become in order to survive and thrive. Huang encouraged open dialogue, inviting his executives to challenge his previous thinking. "The old Jensen wouldn't have considered this idea," he told them. "The new Jensen is open to anything that makes us better."

One of the most important realizations to emerge from this process was the need to expand NVIDIA's vision beyond gaming graphics. While gaming GPUs had been the company's bread and butter, the true future of computing was beginning to take shape in artificial intelligence, deep learning, and data centers. If NVIDIA continued to think of itself solely as a gaming hardware company, it would miss out on a much larger revolution.

So Huang led the charge in shifting NVIDIA's focus. He doubled down on investments in AI and data centers, even as skeptics warned that it was too much of a departure from the company's core identity. He knew the pivot wouldn't yield results overnight, but he was willing to take the risk.

At the same time, he pushed for a reinvention of company culture. The "new Jensen" emphasized agility, risk-taking, and adaptability. He encouraged employees to think like entrepreneurs, to question old assumptions, and to challenge him if they believed he was making the wrong call. It was no longer just about being good at what NVIDIA had always done—it was about being the best at what came next.

The transformation didn't happen overnight, but the results were undeniable. Over the next few years, NVIDIA emerged stronger than ever. The company's early investments in AI and deep learning paid off, turning it into a critical player in a field that would dominate the future of computing. The data center business exploded, and NVIDIA's GPUs became indispensable in everything from autonomous driving to scientific research.

By the late 2010s and early 2020s, NVIDIA was no longer just a graphics company—it was an AI powerhouse. The stock soared, and the company's market cap crossed $1 trillion, a milestone that would have seemed impossible during the struggles that led to Huang's self-firing.

Looking back, the day he "fired himself" wasn't just a bold leadership move—it was a masterclass in humility, self-awareness, and adaptability. It demonstrated that the greatest leaders aren't those who cling to old ways of thinking but those who are willing to challenge themselves, to admit when they need to evolve, and to inspire their teams to do the same.

Today, NVIDIA stands as one of the most influential technology companies in the world, and much of that success can be traced back to a single moment of radical accountability. Jensen Huang didn't wait for the world to force him to change—he forced himself to change first. And in doing so, he transformed not just his own leadership but the future of NVIDIA itself.

WORLD'S FIRST A

Chapter 12: No Bureaucracy, Just Results

In the world of artificial intelligence, speed is everything. The difference between training a deep learning model in a week versus a month can mean the difference between success and stagnation. Few people understand this better than Jensen Huang, the co-founder and CEO of NVIDIA, whose company provides the computing power that fuels modern AI. But Huang doesn't just sell hardware—he makes sure the right people get what they need when they need it, even if that means shipping a supercomputer overnight.

In the mid-2010s, OpenAI was working on pioneering deep learning research that would eventually lead to breakthroughs in AI capabilities, including the development of ChatGPT. At the time, AI research required enormous computational resources, and training models at scale was a logistical and financial challenge. The team at OpenAI needed the best hardware available to keep pushing forward, and there was only one company that could provide it: NVIDIA.

One evening, OpenAI reached out to NVIDIA with an urgent request. They needed more computational power—immediately. Training their latest deep learning models was taking too long, and waiting weeks for new hardware would slow down their progress. Huang, known for his hands-on leadership style, personally got involved. Instead of going through the usual procurement processes, he cut through the red tape and made an unprecedented decision: he arranged for an NVIDIA DGX supercomputer to be shipped overnight to OpenAI's headquarters.

A DGX system wasn't just any piece of hardware. It was one of the most powerful AI machines in existence, equipped with high-performance GPUs optimized for deep learning. At the time, such supercomputers weren't casually sent out overnight. They were expensive, required careful setup, and were in high demand. But Huang saw the bigger picture—AI was on the cusp of revolutionizing the world, and OpenAI was leading the charge. Delaying their research by even a few days wasn't an option.

The logistics of shipping a supercomputer overnight were far from simple. Unlike a consumer product that could be boxed and shipped via standard carriers, an NVIDIA DGX system was a massive, industrial-grade machine requiring specialized handling. Arrangements were made for immediate transport, ensuring that the hardware would arrive safely and be operational as quickly as possible.

The move paid off. OpenAI's team received the system the next day, set it up, and immediately integrated it into their workflow. The additional computing power drastically accelerated their research, allowing them to train their deep learning models at an unprecedented speed. What might have taken months was completed in weeks, pushing OpenAI's research forward at a critical moment.

Huang's decision wasn't just about providing hardware; it was about demonstrating the kind of support that fosters true innovation. By removing obstacles and ensuring OpenAI had what it needed, NVIDIA positioned itself not just as a hardware provider but as a partner in AI progress. The move solidified NVIDIA's relationship with OpenAI and set a precedent for how the company would engage with AI researchers worldwide.

This wasn't an isolated incident. Huang had a track record of making bold, unconventional moves to support AI research. NVIDIA had already established itself as the go-to company for deep learning hardware, but Huang knew that relationships mattered just as much as technology. By personally intervening and making sure OpenAI got what it needed without delay, he demonstrated a level of commitment that few other CEOs could match.

The impact of that overnight shipment was felt far beyond OpenAI's offices. The accelerated research contributed to advancements that would later shape the AI industry, including the development of large language models that now power chatbots, image recognition systems, and other AI applications used by millions. It also reinforced NVIDIA's role as the backbone of modern AI, ensuring that every major breakthrough in the field would, in some way, be tied to their technology.

Today, NVIDIA remains the dominant force in AI computing, and OpenAI continues to push the boundaries of what's possible. But the story of the overnight supercomputer remains a defining moment—a testament to Huang's belief that speed, decisiveness, and support for researchers are just as crucial as the hardware itself. In a world where innovation waits for no one, Huang made sure that OpenAI didn't have to wait either.

The Early Lessons on Efficiency

Jensen Huang never had much patience for bureaucracy. From the earliest days of Nvidia, he saw how excessive layers of management slowed down decision-making, created bottlenecks, and stifled innovation. His vision for the company was different—he wanted Nvidia to be a place where ideas moved quickly from conception to execution, where engineers had the autonomy to do their best work without being mired in red tape. Over the years, he meticulously designed an organizational structure that embodied these principles, rejecting traditional corporate hierarchies in favor of a dynamic, results-driven approach.

Jensen's intolerance for bureaucracy wasn't just an abstract principle—it was forged in the crucible of experience. During his early career at LSI Logic and AMD, he had witnessed firsthand how slow decision-making could kill great ideas before they even had a chance to take off. Projects would get stuck in endless cycles of approvals, meetings would drag on without clear conclusions, and unnecessary managerial oversight would sap the motivation of talented engineers. He learned that speed was not just an advantage; it was a necessity in the fast-moving world of technology.

By the time he co-founded Nvidia in 1993, he was determined to build a company where the best ideas won—not the ideas that had been processed through multiple layers of approval. "If you want to do something extraordinary, you have to create an environment where people can make extraordinary decisions without waiting for permission," he later explained.

One of the most radical decisions Jensen made at Nvidia was to flatten the company's hierarchy. Instead of following the traditional model where information flowed slowly up and down a rigid chain of command, he created a structure where almost everyone in the company had direct access to leadership. He famously maintained over 60 direct reports—a number that would be unthinkable for most CEOs.

The reason was simple: he didn't want managers acting as intermediaries between himself and the people actually doing the work. "I don't need someone to filter information for me," he said. "I want to hear directly from the people who are solving problems every day." By removing layers of middle management, he ensured that decisions could be made faster and with greater clarity.

This approach also meant that Nvidia could pivot quickly in response to technological changes. Unlike traditional companies, where a shift in strategy might take months of meetings and revisions, Nvidia had the ability to realign its efforts almost instantly. This agility became a defining characteristic of the company and a key reason why it was able to stay ahead of competitors in the volatile semiconductor industry.

No One-on-One Meetings, Only Group Discussions

Another unconventional practice Jensen instituted was his refusal to hold one-on-one meetings with his direct reports. Instead, he preferred group discussions where multiple perspectives could be shared at once. This ensured that information flowed freely across the organization and that no single person became a bottleneck.

"If I have to say something important, I want everyone to hear it at the same time," he explained. "That way, there's no misinterpretation, no delay, and no wasted effort repeating the same thing in multiple conversations."

This practice also had a cultural impact. It reinforced the idea that Nvidia was a place where decisions were made collectively and transparently. Employees knew that if they had a great idea, they could present it directly in front of leadership and get immediate feedback. It also fostered a sense of accountability—when everyone is in the same room, it's much harder to pass the buck or shift responsibility.

Fighting Against Corporate Politics

Bureaucracy isn't just about layers of management—it's also about office politics, favoritism, and internal power struggles. Jensen knew that for Nvidia to succeed, he had to eliminate these distractions.

One of the ways he did this was by making it clear that Nvidia was a meritocracy. Promotions weren't based on tenure or who you knew; they were based on results. If someone had a breakthrough idea or demonstrated exceptional leadership, they would be recognized and rewarded—regardless of their title or position within the company.

This approach created an intensely competitive but highly productive culture. Employees knew that their work mattered and that they weren't just cogs in a machine. It also meant that Nvidia attracted some of the best talent in the industry—engineers and designers who were passionate about their work and wanted to be part of a company that valued innovation over politics.

The Speed Factor: Making Decisions at the Pace of Innovation

Jensen often spoke about the importance of making decisions quickly. "In technology, if you're not moving fast, you're dead," he once said. This philosophy guided every aspect of Nvidia's operations. Unlike many large corporations that operated on quarterly or yearly planning cycles, Nvidia worked in real time. If a new opportunity emerged or if a project needed to be adjusted, the company could respond immediately.

A perfect example of this came in the early 2010s when Jensen saw the potential for GPUs to power artificial intelligence. At the time, Nvidia was still primarily known as a gaming company. But rather than going through endless committees and strategic planning sessions, Jensen made the call almost unilaterally: Nvidia would pivot aggressively into AI.

This decision, made with speed and conviction, turned out to be one of the most significant in Nvidia's history. Today, Nvidia is a leader in AI computing, and that success can be traced back to Jensen's refusal to let bureaucracy slow down the company's ability to act.

A Company Built on Results

Ultimately, Jensen's approach to management comes down to one thing: results. He doesn't care about titles, procedures, or corporate formalities. What he cares about is whether Nvidia is producing groundbreaking technology and staying ahead of the competition.

"We're not here to follow rules," he told his team. "We're here to invent the future."

This mindset has made Nvidia one of the most innovative and fastest-growing companies in the world. While other companies get bogged down in bureaucracy, Nvidia moves forward with relentless focus and speed. And at the center of it all is Jensen Huang, a leader who has proven time and again that in a world driven by technology, bureaucracy is a luxury that no company can afford.

Chapter 13: The Customer is the North Star

In the world of PC gaming and custom builds, few things are more prized than a high-performance GPU. For modders, enthusiasts, and tech creators, a powerful graphics card isn't just a piece of hardware—it's the heart of their machines, the key to unlocking stunning visuals and peak performance. Among these passionate builders, one individual found themselves at the center of an unbelievable moment—one where their craftsmanship was not only noticed by NVIDIA's legendary CEO, Jensen Huang, but personally rewarded in a way they never could have imagined.

The Hand-Delivered GPU

It all started with a simple post online. A dedicated PC modder, known in the enthusiast community for their intricate builds and meticulous attention to detail, unveiled a custom NVIDIA-themed rig. This wasn't just any gaming PC—it was a masterclass in design, featuring an all-black, futuristic aesthetic that paid homage to NVIDIA's branding, complete with green LED lighting and intricate cooling systems that looked straight out of a sci-fi film. The build was optimized for performance, equipped with high-end components, liquid cooling, and modifications that pushed the boundaries of PC craftsmanship.

The images went viral among the modding and gaming communities, with enthusiasts praising the builder's dedication. Comments flooded in, admiring the rig's aesthetic and its seamless integration of NVIDIA's signature branding. But among the thousands of people who saw it, one stood out: Jensen Huang himself.

Huang, known for his deep engagement with the NVIDIA fanbase, frequently keeps an eye on community forums, tech threads, and social media posts that showcase innovative uses of his company's technology. Unlike many corporate executives who remain distant from their customers, Huang has always had a hands-on approach—personally responding to developers, AI researchers, and even everyday gamers who show passion for NVIDIA products.

When Huang came across the stunning build, he was immediately taken aback. Here was a fan, a creator, who had taken the essence of NVIDIA and transformed it into a piece of art. Rather than merely liking or reposting the image, Huang decided to go one step further—he wanted to personally reward the creator.

The Surprise of a Lifetime

The modder had no idea what was coming. A few days after their post had gone viral, they received an unexpected message: NVIDIA wanted to get in touch. At first, they assumed it was just routine PR or fan engagement. But when they were told that Jensen Huang himself had taken a personal interest in their work, they were in disbelief.

Then came the real shocker. Huang wasn't just offering praise—he was sending them something unprecedented. NVIDIA had been developing an unreleased, one-of-a-kind custom GPU, a prototype model with cutting-edge features that had yet to be seen by the public. It wasn't available for sale, wasn't part of any known product line, and had never been featured in a keynote. It was a piece of next-generation technology, and Huang wanted this modder to have it.

Alongside the GPU, Huang included something even more personal—a handwritten note. "Your passion, creativity, and dedication inspire us. This belongs to you. Keep pushing boundaries." It was signed simply: "Jensen."

Most people would expect a package like this to arrive via courier or be shipped discreetly. But Huang, ever the unconventional leader, had something else in mind. Since he was traveling near the region, he decided to personally hand-deliver the GPU himself.

When the modder opened their door to find Jensen Huang standing there, leather jacket and all, holding a package, they were speechless. "I just wanted to say thank you," Huang said with a smile, handing over the box. It was a surreal moment—one that instantly became legendary within the gaming and tech communities.

The modder, struggling to find words, invited Huang inside to take a closer look at the build that had caught his attention. Huang examined every detail, asking about the custom modifications, the cooling system, and the thought process behind the design. Their conversation wasn't about business—it was about passion, about the craft of building something special.

The news of this extraordinary encounter spread like wildfire. Forums exploded with discussions, gamers speculated on the specifications of the mysterious GPU, and other modders expressed their excitement (and a bit of envy). NVIDIA fans saw it as yet another testament to Huang's unique leadership style—one that blurred the lines between CEO and enthusiast, making him one of the most respected figures in the industry.

Beyond the excitement of receiving unreleased hardware, the modder was left with something even more valuable: recognition. In an industry where individual creators often go unnoticed, Huang's gesture sent a powerful message—passion and creativity matter. NVIDIA wasn't just about products; it was about the people who used them to create, innovate, and push technology forward.

The custom GPU, once a prototype hidden from the world, became the centerpiece of the modder's build. They shared their experience online, not just showcasing the card but also emphasizing what the moment had meant to them. It wasn't about the hardware—it was about feeling seen, feeling valued by the company and the person at its helm.

For NVIDIA, the moment wasn't just a publicity win—it was a reinforcement of its core philosophy. The company thrived because of its community: the developers, the researchers, the gamers, and the modders who used NVIDIA's technology to bring their ideas to life. Recognizing and rewarding that passion was part of what made NVIDIA more than just a tech company—it made it a movement.

Huang's decision to hand-deliver a GPU wasn't about grand gestures—it was about staying connected. It was about acknowledging that some of the best innovations don't happen in corporate R&D labs, but in the hands of the people who love technology enough to make it their art. And in that moment, standing in a small room with a passionate creator, Jensen Huang once again proved why he wasn't just leading a company—he was leading a revolution.

Knowing the Customers Better Than They Knew Themselves

In the earliest days of Nvidia, after the failure of their first product, the NV1, Jensen had a revelation. The graphics chip, though ambitious, had been too complex, offering features customers didn't ask for. The market simply wanted a faster and more efficient graphics card. This failure nearly killed Nvidia, but instead of retreating, Jensen dissected the failure meticulously.

"We learned it was better to do fewer things well than to do too many things," he later reflected. This painful lesson would define Nvidia's approach for decades to come. From that moment, every product Nvidia developed had to pass one test: Does this solve a real problem for our customers?

Jensen Huang's obsession with customer needs was not just a business strategy; it was a philosophy, a guiding principle that shaped Nvidia's trajectory from a scrappy startup to a dominant force in computing. Unlike many tech visionaries who built products first and sought customers later, Jensen insisted on designing products with a deep understanding of what customers actually needed, even when they themselves did not yet realize it.

Jensen understood that the most groundbreaking products often solved problems customers hadn't fully articulated yet. This required Nvidia to anticipate the future by staying deeply embedded in its customers' world. He would frequently visit gaming studios, data centers, and research labs, listening to engineers, developers, and IT managers, absorbing their frustrations and dreams.

One such visit to a gaming studio in the late 1990s proved pivotal. Developers were frustrated by the limitations of existing graphics technology. They didn't need a Swiss army knife of features; they needed raw power, fast rendering speeds, and reliability. Jensen internalized this frustration and channeled it into what became the GeForce 256—the world's first graphics processing unit (GPU).

By focusing on what game developers truly needed, rather than what Nvidia engineers thought was cool, Jensen steered Nvidia into dominance in the gaming industry. The GeForce line of GPUs became synonymous with cutting-edge gaming technology, a direct result of Jensen's relentless commitment to serving his customers' most pressing needs.

AI and the Expanding Customer Base

While gaming had established Nvidia as a leader in graphics technology, Jensen saw an even greater opportunity on the horizon—one that customers themselves were just beginning to explore: artificial intelligence.

Around 2012, a small group of researchers had begun experimenting with Nvidia's GPUs to accelerate deep learning algorithms. Traditional CPUs struggled to process the massive amounts of data required for AI training, but Nvidia's GPUs excelled at parallel processing, making them an ideal tool for AI researchers. When Jensen learned about this, he didn't dismiss it as a niche use case. Instead, he realized that AI would redefine computing itself.

Rather than waiting for the market to develop, Jensen proactively shifted Nvidia's strategy. He poured billions into building CUDA, a software platform that enabled AI developers to fully harness Nvidia's hardware. Critics thought he was overinvesting in a market that didn't yet exist, but Jensen knew better. He knew because he had listened to the researchers, the developers, the visionaries at the forefront of AI.

By the time AI exploded into mainstream adoption, Nvidia was not just ready—it was the undisputed leader. Companies like Google, Facebook, and Tesla turned to Nvidia to power their AI systems, and Nvidia's GPUs became the gold standard for machine learning. Once again, Jensen had anticipated what customers needed before they even fully realized it themselves.

Direct Engagement

Unlike many CEOs who relied on intermediaries to understand customers, Jensen maintained a hands-on approach. He would often walk into meetings with engineers and customers unannounced, engaging in deep technical discussions, sketching out ideas on whiteboards, and challenging assumptions. His method was not to dictate but to listen, absorb, and then act with precision.

One engineer at a major automotive company recalled an interaction with Jensen during Nvidia's early days in self-driving technology. "He walked into the meeting, asked a few questions, then grabbed a marker and started mapping out a solution right there on the whiteboard. It wasn't just talk—he understood our challenges at a fundamental level. That's why we trusted him."

This kind of direct engagement wasn't limited to major clients. At Nvidia's annual GPU Technology Conference (GTC), Jensen would personally answer questions from students, startup founders, and independent developers. He understood that the best ideas didn't always come from the biggest customers; sometimes, they came from the most passionate users.

Nvidia's rapid product development cycle was another testament to Jensen's customer-centric approach. Feedback loops were built directly into the company's operations. Customers weren't just end users; they were co-creators.

For instance, when Nvidia released its early AI chips, researchers provided feedback on bottlenecks in performance. Rather than waiting for the next product cycle, Jensen's team iterated aggressively, pushing out software updates that significantly improved efficiency. This responsiveness turned Nvidia into not just a vendor, but a trusted partner in innovation.

Even as Nvidia expanded into new industries—healthcare, autonomous vehicles, and cloud computing—the company maintained this relentless focus on solving real customer problems. Jensen often repeated a simple mantra to his team: "If we don't serve the customer, someone else will."

Jensen's philosophy of obsessive customer focus continues to shape Nvidia's future. With AI becoming a fundamental part of industries ranging from medicine to finance, Nvidia's roadmap is not just about technological breakthroughs—it's about ensuring that those breakthroughs align with what customers need most.

As Jensen often says, "Our mission is not to make chips. Our mission is to make our customers successful." This ethos has turned Nvidia into more than a hardware company—it has become an indispensable partner to businesses and innovators worldwide.

Chapter 14: A Culture of Relentless Innovation

Jensen Huang had always believed that a company's greatest strength lay not just in its leadership but in its people—particularly their ability to think independently, solve difficult problems, and push boundaries. At Nvidia, innovation was not confined to a research lab or a select group of individuals; it was ingrained in the DNA of every employee. From the company's earliest days, Huang sought to build an environment where employees were empowered to take risks, propose radical ideas, and challenge conventions without fear of failure.

Thinkers, Not Just Doers

Huang never wanted Nvidia to be just another technology company; he wanted it to be a place where the best minds in the world converged to invent the future. In his view, innovation wasn't something that happened sporadically—it had to be systematic, deliberate, and continuous. To ensure this, he established what he called a "perpetual startup culture," where even as Nvidia grew into a multi-billion-dollar enterprise, it retained the agility and urgency of a fledgling company.

To achieve this, Huang emphasized decentralized decision-making. He didn't want layers of bureaucracy slowing down progress. Instead, he encouraged engineers, designers, and researchers to take ownership of their ideas, experiment with new technologies, and explore solutions without waiting for top-down approval. The Whiteboard, a central tool in Nvidia's culture, played a key role in this. Employees were expected to demonstrate their thought process in real time, often presenting ideas in impromptu discussions where senior executives, including Huang himself, would engage in rigorous debates.

"If you can't explain your idea clearly on a Whiteboard, then you haven't thought it through," Huang often told his employees. It wasn't just about having ideas; it was about refining them through scrutiny, iteration, and discussion. The best ideas, he believed, would naturally survive this rigorous environment and rise to the top.

A crucial element of Nvidia's innovation culture was its tolerance for failure. Huang knew that breakthroughs didn't come from playing it safe. If a company truly wanted to push the boundaries of what was possible, it had to be willing to take big risks. He admired how companies like Apple, Tesla, and

Amazon had bet their futures on ambitious, seemingly impossible ideas—and succeeded.

He often reminded his employees of the failures Nvidia had endured in its early years, particularly with the NV1, the company's first graphics processor, which flopped in the market. Instead of treating the failure as a setback, Huang used it as a learning opportunity. The team dissected every mistake, identified what went wrong, and applied those lessons to future designs. This mindset became deeply embedded in Nvidia's culture: Fail fast, learn faster, and keep moving forward.

Employees were encouraged to pursue experimental projects without the fear that failure would cost them their careers. In fact, some of Nvidia's biggest successes came from ideas that initially seemed too risky. The company's pivot into artificial intelligence (AI) is a prime example. When Huang and his team began exploring the use of GPUs for AI and deep learning, the idea was met with skepticism from many in the industry. At the time, GPUs were primarily used for gaming, and few believed they could revolutionize machine learning. But Huang saw potential where others saw improbability. He supported teams working on deep learning applications, investing resources into AI research even before the market recognized its value. The result? Nvidia became the leader in AI hardware, powering everything from self-driving cars to advanced language models.

Encouraging Intellectual Freedom

Huang also believed that innovation couldn't be forced—it had to be inspired. That meant creating an environment where employees felt free to explore new ideas without constant managerial oversight. One of the ways he did this was by encouraging informal collaboration across different teams. At Nvidia, engineers from different departments were encouraged to share their projects, seek feedback from colleagues, and even propose ideas outside their direct areas of expertise.

This cross-pollination of ideas led to some of Nvidia's most groundbreaking developments. The CUDA (Compute Unified Device Architecture) platform, which transformed Nvidia's GPUs into powerful parallel processors for scientific computing, was born out of an internal experiment. Engineers who were initially working on gaming applications began to see how GPUs could be repurposed for high-performance computing. Instead of shutting down the idea because it deviated from Nvidia's core business, Huang embraced it—and CUDA became a key driver of Nvidia's expansion into AI, data science, and supercomputing.

Huang also took a hands-on approach to nurturing talent. He would often walk the hallways, dropping into meetings unannounced, engaging with employees about their projects, and offering suggestions or challenges. His presence wasn't intimidating—it was energizing. Employees saw him as someone who genuinely cared about their work, and they felt empowered to contribute to the company's larger mission.

One of the most unique aspects of Nvidia's innovation culture was what employees jokingly referred to as its "Skunk Works" projects—high-risk, high-reward initiatives that were given the freedom to operate outside the traditional corporate structure. These projects weren't just about making incremental improvements; they were about pursuing disruptive innovations that could redefine entire industries.

One such project was Nvidia's venture into the automotive industry. When Huang announced that Nvidia would be developing AI-driven computing for autonomous vehicles, many thought it was a strange pivot. After all, Nvidia was a graphics company, not a car manufacturer. But Huang saw the long-term potential in AI-powered transportation and bet big on the idea. He assembled a team of experts, gave them the resources they needed, and let them operate with minimal interference. The result? Nvidia's DRIVE platform became one of the most advanced autonomous driving systems in the world, used by companies like Tesla, Mercedes-Benz, and Toyota.

Another example was Nvidia's foray into the metaverse with Omniverse, a platform that allows developers to create and simulate virtual worlds. While many companies were still trying to figure out what the metaverse even meant, Nvidia had already built the tools to bring it to life. This ability to anticipate the future and invest in ideas ahead of the market was a direct result of Huang's innovation-first mindset.

For Huang, the ultimate goal wasn't just to innovate within Nvidia but to create a generation of innovators who would continue pushing the company forward. He invested heavily in mentorship programs, ensuring that young engineers had access to Nvidia's top minds. He also promoted an internal culture where experience didn't dictate influence—new employees, regardless of age or tenure, were encouraged to speak up and challenge ideas.

Huang was particularly passionate about expanding opportunities for students and researchers. Nvidia regularly collaborated with universities, funding AI research labs and providing grants to students working on cutting-edge technologies. Huang knew that some of the best ideas came from the academic world, and he wanted Nvidia to be a bridge between theoretical research and real-world application.

Perhaps the most defining characteristic of Huang's approach to internal innovation was his refusal to settle. No matter how successful Nvidia became, he always saw more work to be done. He often quoted the phrase, "We are always 30 days away from going out of business," a reminder that complacency was the enemy of progress.

Even as Nvidia became one of the most valuable technology companies in the world, Huang remained just as hungry as he was in the early days. He encouraged employees to constantly ask themselves: "What's next?" The goal was never to simply maintain Nvidia's position at the top, but to continue reinventing the company, disrupting itself before anyone else could.

For Huang, innovation wasn't just a business strategy—it was a way of life. And under his leadership, Nvidia would continue to be a company where the impossible was simply the starting point.

Chapter 15: The CEO Who Games – And Wins

Most CEOs talk about their products, but few actually use them the way their customers do. Jensen Huang, however, is not most CEOs. As the co-founder and CEO of NVIDIA, the company that revolutionized gaming graphics, he doesn't just oversee the development of cutting-edge gaming hardware—he plays with it. And not just casually. Huang is a serious gamer, one who believes that in order to build the best gaming hardware in the world, you have to know what gamers need. And sometimes, that means proving it in the most direct way possible: by utterly humiliating his own employees in a multiplayer showdown.

Jensen Huang's reputation in the tech industry is one of visionary leadership and relentless innovation. But what many don't realize is that his connection to gaming isn't just professional—it's personal. Long before NVIDIA became a trillion-dollar company, Huang was deeply immersed in gaming culture, appreciating not only the technology behind it but the thrill of competition itself.

While other executives might tout gaming as a market segment, for Huang, it's a passion. He understands the frustrations of lag, the need for high frame rates, and the difference between an average and an exceptional gaming experience. And unlike many CEOs who rely on second-hand reports or analysts to understand their customers, Huang prefers a more hands-on approach—by picking up a controller or sitting at a high-end gaming PC himself.

At an internal NVIDIA event, employees gathered for what was supposed to be a fun, friendly multiplayer gaming tournament. It was an opportunity for developers and engineers to unwind, to test out the very products they had helped create. The atmosphere was electric—employees were eager to showcase their skills, and among them were some of the most knowledgeable minds in gaming technology.

Then came the surprise.

Midway through the event, Huang stepped forward and challenged his employees to a match. There was a mixture of excitement and nervous laughter. No one had expected the CEO to participate—after all, how many executives at his level actually game? But Huang was dead serious.

"Let's see if you guys are as good at playing as you are at designing," he said with a grin.

What followed was nothing short of legendary.

The game of choice? A fast-paced, high-skill multiplayer shooter that required precision, reflexes, and strategic thinking. Employees assumed that, at best, Huang would hold his own for a few rounds before getting overwhelmed by players who spent their free time perfecting their skills.

They were wrong.

Huang didn't just compete—he dominated. From the moment the match began, he displayed the kind of skill that only comes from years of gaming experience. His movements were precise, his aim impeccable, and his strategic awareness unparalleled. One by one, employees fell, unable to match his speed and decision-making. The scoreboard told the story: Huang wasn't just winning—he was crushing the competition.

As the match went on, disbelief turned to respect. Employees who had initially underestimated their CEO now realized they were dealing with a formidable opponent. The room, once filled with chatter, grew quieter as people focused on trying to take him down. But no matter how hard they tried, Huang stayed ahead, racking up kill streaks and delivering headshot after headshot.

Then came his now-iconic remark: "If you can't beat me, how are you going to design the best gaming hardware?"

It was half-joking, half-serious—but the message was clear. If NVIDIA was going to continue leading the gaming industry, its engineers, developers, and designers had to think like gamers, play like gamers, and truly understand what made a great gaming experience.

When the match finally ended, Huang stood up, stretched, and laughed. "Not bad," he said, "but you've got work to do."

The employees, though humbled, were energized. Losing to their CEO wasn't a disappointment—it was a revelation. If the person at the top of the company could engage with their technology at this level, then they had no excuse not to strive for excellence. Huang's performance wasn't just about bragging rights; it was about setting a standard.

From that day forward, stories of the NVIDIA showdown spread throughout the company. It became one of those legendary moments—an event that captured the essence of what made NVIDIA unique. It wasn't just a company building GPUs; it was a company led by people who genuinely loved gaming, who understood the needs of their users, and who demanded nothing less than the best.

This wasn't an isolated incident. Huang continued to engage with the gaming community, participating in internal playtests, offering feedback on performance, and keeping up with gaming trends. He encouraged his teams to play, to experiment, and to always think about the end user's experience. Under his leadership, NVIDIA's gaming division flourished, producing groundbreaking advancements like real-time ray tracing, DLSS (Deep Learning Super Sampling), and AI-driven enhancements that redefined what was possible in gaming graphics.

And, of course, employees never forgot the day they went head-to-head with their CEO—and lost. For many, it was a reminder that at NVIDIA, gaming wasn't just business; it was personal.

The Lasting Impact

Today, NVIDIA stands as the dominant force in gaming hardware, supplying GPUs for everything from high-end gaming rigs to next-generation consoles. But its success isn't just due to cutting-edge engineering—it's built on a culture of passion, one where the CEO himself leads by example.

Jensen Huang's infamous gaming showdown wasn't about proving superiority—it was about demonstrating the mindset required to lead an industry. His message was clear: If you want to design the best gaming hardware in the world, you have to live and breathe gaming yourself. And as long as he's at the helm, that's exactly what NVIDIA will continue to do.

Speed of Light

One of his engineers recalled a meeting where Jensen was reviewing an upcoming graphics chip design. The team had projected a timeline of two years before the product would be market-ready. Jensen simply shook his head. "We have twelve months," he said. "Find a way. If we don't get there first, it doesn't matter how great it is." No one argued with him, because history had proven him right time and again. Under his leadership, Nvidia had consistently released groundbreaking products faster than its competitors, establishing itself as an industry leader in GPUs and later, AI computing.

Those who worked closely with Jensen at Nvidia often spoke of his relentless pace. Meetings started and ended at precise times, with no tolerance for meandering discussions. If an employee hesitated in their response, Jensen would move on to someone else. If a project lagged, it was restructured immediately. "We move at the speed of light here," he once told his executives, "because if we don't, we're already dead."

Jensen believed that speed was not just about cutting corners—it was about discipline, execution, and anticipation. He structured Nvidia's workflow to reduce inefficiencies at every level. The company operated with a famously flat hierarchy, eliminating bureaucratic bottlenecks that slowed decision-making.

When Jensen made a decision, it was executed immediately. No waiting for approvals, no endless rounds of refinement. He encouraged employees to act first and iterate later. If an idea failed, it was discarded quickly. If it worked, it was scaled aggressively. This bias for action became the foundation of Nvidia's success.

Jensen was fond of telling his engineers, "Don't bring me problems—bring me solutions." His leadership style was not for everyone, but for those who thrived under pressure, it was exhilarating. The pace at Nvidia was punishing, but it also meant that ideas turned into reality at a speed rarely seen in the tech industry. "We do things here in months that other companies take years to accomplish," Jensen once said. "And that is why we win."

One of the most defining examples of Jensen's speed-driven mindset was Nvidia's pivot toward artificial intelligence. In the early 2010s, while the rest of the tech world was still focused on traditional computing, Jensen saw the future in deep learning. He understood that GPUs, originally designed for gaming, were uniquely suited for the complex computations needed for AI training.

Most companies would have hesitated, waiting for the market to confirm the opportunity. Not Nvidia. Jensen pushed Nvidia's engineers to start optimizing their hardware for AI before the industry had even realized it needed it. "We're not waiting for permission," he said in a meeting. "AI is coming, and when it does, we will be ready."

The gamble paid off spectacularly. By the time AI became the hottest trend in Silicon Valley, Nvidia was already years ahead, with its GPUs being the gold standard for machine learning applications. It was not luck; it was speed. Speed of vision, speed of execution, speed of delivery.

Jensen's insistence on rapid execution often meant asking for what seemed impossible. But he did not believe in limitations. "If we don't do it, someone else will," he often reminded his team. He had an uncanny ability to push people beyond their own perceived limits.

A former Nvidia executive once shared a story about the development of the company's first AI-optimized GPU. Engineers had spent months on the project, only for Jensen to call a last-minute review and announce that they needed to double the chip's efficiency—without pushing the release date. The team protested. It wasn't possible. The timeline was already tight, and they had stretched every resource.

Two weeks later, they had found a way. They had worked around the clock, solving problems they hadn't even considered before. Jensen's unrelenting demands forced them to be better than they thought they could be. It was brutal, but it worked.

The Cost of Speed

There was a downside to Jensen's obsession with speed. It created an environment where only the toughest survived. The pressure to deliver was immense, and burnout was common. Turnover among employees who couldn't handle the intensity was high. Nvidia wasn't for everyone, and Jensen didn't pretend otherwise.

"This isn't a place for people who like to take their time," he once told a new group of hires. "We do things fast here. If that excites you, you're in the right place. If it scares you, you should probably leave now."

Some did leave, unable to keep up with the pace. But those who stayed became part of a culture that thrived on rapid innovation. They built products that redefined entire industries, from gaming to AI to autonomous driving. They didn't just work fast; they worked smart, anticipating shifts in technology and acting before the world caught on.

Even as Nvidia grew into a multi-billion-dollar tech giant, Jensen never allowed complacency to set in. He continued to push the company to move faster, to think bigger. "We haven't even started," he told his executives in a recent meeting. "The future moves fast. We have to move faster."

That mindset ensured that Nvidia remained not just relevant, but dominant. While competitors played catch-up, Nvidia was already working on the next big thing. Whether it was AI, cloud computing, or quantum graphics, Jensen was already there, pushing the boundaries before anyone else even realized where they needed to be.

Conclusion

Jensen Huang built Nvidia with the philosophy that speed is the ultimate weapon. In an industry where innovation moves at breakneck pace, he ensured that Nvidia always moved faster. He believed that if you hesitated, if you waited, if you second-guessed, you were already behind.

His obsession with speed created one of the most formidable technology companies in the world. It shaped Nvidia's DNA, turning it into an organization that could pivot, adapt, and execute with unprecedented velocity. And as long as Jensen Huang is at the helm, Nvidia will continue to operate at the speed of light, leaving the rest of the world struggling to keep up.

Chapter 16: The Man Behind the CEO

Jensen Huang is a man of many talents. He is a visionary in the tech world, a relentless cyclist, and an engineer at heart. But perhaps one of his most cherished skills lies far from the world of silicon and algorithms. In the warmth of his home kitchen, surrounded by the scent of simmering broth and freshly chopped ingredients, he transforms into something else entirely—a master chef, a creator of flavors, a man who can bring his family together with a single dish.

Cooking, for Jensen, is more than just a hobby. It is a passion, a discipline, and a way to connect with his roots. Despite his demanding schedule running Nvidia, he makes time to cook, often crafting meals that rival those of professional chefs. His specialty? Taiwanese cuisine, the food of his childhood, the flavors that remind him of home.

Among all the dishes he prepares, one stands out: his beef noodle soup. This is not just any soup; it is a dish that has been perfected over years of experimentation, trial, and refinement. According to his family, no restaurant's version comes close to matching his. The broth is rich, deep, layered with spices and slow-cooked for hours to achieve perfection. The noodles are tender yet firm, the beef melts effortlessly, and the combination of flavors is something only a true craftsman could create.

Jensen approaches cooking the same way he approaches leadership—meticulously, with attention to every detail. He sources the best ingredients, believing that quality starts at the foundation. He doesn't rush the process, understanding that patience is key to bringing out the best in a dish. And, just like in his professional life, he never settles for mediocrity. If a dish isn't perfect, he tweaks it, refines it, and makes it better the next time.

His family, used to his culinary excellence, has developed a certain reluctance to eat out. Why go to a restaurant when Jensen's cooking is better? They know that when he steps into the kitchen, the meal will be something extraordinary. It is a testament to his skill that those closest to him—who could choose any high-end dining experience—would rather sit at their own table, eating the food he has lovingly prepared.

Those who have been lucky enough to taste his cooking say that he brings the same intensity to his dishes as he does to Nvidia. He is methodical, precise, yet creative, always finding ways to enhance the experience. His cooking is never rushed, never careless. It is a form of artistry, a reflection of the way he sees the world—not just as a place of business, but as a place of experience, culture, and deep personal connection.

For Jensen, food is more than sustenance. It is a form of storytelling. Each dish carries a memory, a history, a piece of who he is. When he prepares beef noodle soup, he is not just making a meal; he is recreating a part of his past, sharing something deeply personal with those he loves.

His ability to cook at such a high level is impressive given the demands on his time. Running one of the most influential technology companies in the world is no small feat. Yet, amidst all of it, he carves out space for cooking. It is not an afterthought but an essential part of his life.

Perhaps that is what makes Jensen Huang so extraordinary. He is a man who excels in every arena he enters—not just in business, but in the simple, meaningful moments of everyday life. He understands that greatness is not just about innovation and success; it is about taking time to create something beautiful, whether that be a world-changing technology or a perfect bowl of beef noodle soup.

And so, in the quiet of his home, away from the flashing lights and the industry accolades, Jensen Huang stands at his stove, stirring, tasting, adjusting. He is in his element, not as a CEO or a tech mogul, but as a man who loves to cook, who finds joy in the simplest yet most profound of human experiences—sharing a meal with those he loves.

The Cinema Enthusiast

Jensen Huang is a man of precision and discipline, known for his sharp mind and relentless work ethic. But beyond the tech world, where he has built Nvidia into a global powerhouse, there exists another side of him—one that is drawn to the magic of storytelling, the artistry of film, and the boundless worlds created on the silver screen. For Jensen, movies are more than just entertainment; they are a source of inspiration, a way to unwind, and, in many ways, an extension of his passion for technology and creativity.

His love for movies is not confined to a single genre or region. Unlike casual moviegoers who stick to familiar Hollywood blockbusters, Jensen's cinematic tastes are vast and eclectic. He watches everything—from mind-bending science fiction to thought-provoking indie films, from action-packed thrillers to heartwarming Bollywood epics. His curiosity extends to international cinema, appreciating the unique storytelling styles of different cultures. Whether it's a classic from Akira Kurosawa, a European art film, or a groundbreaking anime from Japan, Jensen watches with the same enthusiasm and keen eye for detail that he applies to his work at Nvidia.

Science fiction, in particular, holds a special place in his heart. The genre's ability to push the boundaries of imagination aligns with his own ambitions in the tech industry. Films like Blade Runner, The Matrix, and Interstellar have not only entertained him but have also influenced his vision for the future of computing. The seamless fusion of artificial intelligence, visual effects, and digital storytelling in these films mirrors the work Nvidia does in revolutionizing AI, gaming, and film production technology. It is no coincidence that many of the most visually stunning films of recent years have been powered by Nvidia's advancements in graphics processing and deep learning.

But his appreciation extends beyond the sleek visuals of Hollywood blockbusters. He has spoken about his admiration for Bollywood films, which are known for their emotional depth, vibrant storytelling, and elaborate musical sequences. While some might see Bollywood as merely a spectacle of song and dance, Jensen recognizes the industry's ability to craft compelling narratives that resonate with audiences worldwide. He appreciates the boldness of Bollywood directors who blend drama, action, romance, and music into a single film—something Western cinema often struggles to achieve. Some of his favorite Indian films include 3 Idiots, Lagaan, and Gully Boy, all of which tell powerful stories about perseverance, ambition, and defying expectations—themes that align closely with his own journey in the tech world.

For Jensen, the storytelling in films offers insights into human emotion, ambition, and struggle—key components that drive innovation. He believes that understanding human experiences is crucial in designing technology that improves lives. Nvidia's collaborations with animation and film studios have been directly influenced by his passion for cinema. By pushing the limits of what's possible in digital rendering and real-time graphics, Nvidia has played an essential role in the evolution of visual effects, enabling filmmakers to bring their most ambitious visions to life.

His fascination with movies extends to the people behind the scenes as well. He has a deep respect for directors, cinematographers, and visual effects artists, often comparing their dedication to storytelling with his own team's dedication to engineering breakthroughs. Just as a director must orchestrate an entire production, balancing artistic vision with technical precision, so too must a tech leader like Jensen navigate the ever-evolving world of innovation.

Even with his demanding schedule, he finds time to watch films regularly, often sharing his insights with those around him. He has been known to recommend movies to his colleagues, discussing their themes and production techniques with the same passion he applies to technology. It is this ability to draw connections between art and science, creativity and engineering, that makes him a truly unique leader.

Ultimately, Jensen Huang's love for cinema is not just about entertainment—it is about seeing the world through different lenses, understanding diverse perspectives, and finding inspiration in unexpected places. His appreciation for film influences the way he leads Nvidia, driving the company to continually push the boundaries of what is possible in both technology and storytelling. Whether it's the breathtaking landscapes of a sci-fi epic or the emotionally charged journey of a Bollywood drama, every film he watches adds another layer to his ever-expanding vision for the future.

The CEO and His Cat

Jensen Huang is known for commanding a room, for leading thousands of engineers, and for driving Nvidia to the forefront of technological innovation. But in his own home, there is one creature that holds the ultimate veto power—a cat with an attitude problem.

Unlike the many engineers and executives who respect Huang for his vision and leadership, this particular feline operates on an entirely different wavelength. The cat, whose name has been kept a family secret, is notorious for its aloof nature, its disdain for guests, and its complete disregard for anyone in the household—except for Jensen.

Huang's family and friends often joke about the cat's behavior, pointing out that it seems to have adopted the same discerning, high-standard mentality as its owner. It is not easily impressed, it does not seek approval, and it does not entertain small talk. Much like Jensen in the boardroom, the cat seems to recognize value in efficiency and direct engagement. It wastes no time on anyone it deems unworthy of attention. And yet, for all its hostility toward others, it has an undeniable, almost reverent respect for Huang.

Family members recount countless stories of how guests have tried and failed to win the cat's favor. Some approach with food, others with toys. A few optimists even attempt gentle coaxing. The cat's response is always the same—a sharp glare, an unimpressed flick of the tail, and, if pressed further, a decisive hiss. But when Jensen enters the room, the transformation is instantaneous. The once-rebellious feline softens, pads over to him, and curls up at his feet or on his lap, as if acknowledging that in this household, he alone is worthy of its loyalty.

For Huang, who has spent decades leading and inspiring some of the brightest minds in technology, the dynamic is both amusing and affirming. Leadership, after all, isn't about forcing compliance—it's about earning respect. And if even a notoriously difficult cat recognizes his authority, then surely that says something about his natural ability to lead.

Some have speculated that the cat's unique preference for Jensen is due to his calm and composed demeanor. Unlike others who approach the cat with a need for affection or validation, Huang treats it much like he treats his work—patiently, strategically, and with an understanding that respect is not given lightly. Perhaps the cat sees in him a kindred spirit—someone who values loyalty, efficiency, and, above all, results.

Huang himself has never claimed to have any special animal-training skills. He doesn't make exaggerated efforts to bond with the cat, nor does he attempt to control its behavior. Instead, much like he does in his professional life, he allows respect to develop naturally. He recognizes the cat's independence, its personality, and its unwillingness to conform for the sake of others.

Despite its aloof nature, the cat has become an integral part of the Huang household. Family members have accepted its selective favoritism, often watching in amusement as it snubs their attempts at affection while immediately responding to Jensen's quiet presence. It has become something of an inside joke within the family—an unspoken understanding that even the pet of the house adheres to a hierarchy that places Huang at the top.

This peculiar dynamic has led to countless dinner table conversations and humorous anecdotes. Friends visiting the Huang residence are often forewarned: "Don't take it personally if the cat ignores you. It only listens to Jensen." And sure enough, they witness firsthand the cat's sharp disinterest in everyone but its chosen human.

Huang, ever the pragmatist, finds the entire situation amusing but unsurprising. In his view, respect is something that must be earned, not demanded. And if a cat, of all creatures, understands this principle, then perhaps there's a lesson to be learned in leadership—one that transcends the world of business and extends into the simple, everyday relationships that define life at home.

In the end, the cat remains a mystery to everyone but Jensen. While the rest of the family may never win its favor, they have come to accept and even admire the peculiar bond between the CEO and his feline companion. It is, in many ways, a perfect representation of Huang's life—surrounded by people, respected by many, yet truly understood and followed by only a select few.

And so, while Nvidia continues to push the boundaries of artificial intelligence and computational power, back at home, one small but fierce creature ensures that Jensen Huang's leadership is still recognized, even beyond the walls of his company.

Chapter 17: The Long Game

Jensen Huang never played for short-term wins. He built for the long term, playing a game where patience and perseverance determined the ultimate outcome. His ability to think decades ahead, endure periods of struggle, and commit to a vision before the rest of the world recognized its value set him apart. If there was one thing that defined Huang's leadership, it was his unwavering belief in the long horizon.

Betting on the Future

When Huang co-founded Nvidia in 1993 with Chris Malachowsky and Curtis Priem, the world had barely begun to explore the potential of graphics processing units (GPUs). Most of the industry focused on central processing units (CPUs) as the backbone of computing, but Huang saw something different. He understood that graphics chips, which were being used primarily for video games, had the potential to revolutionize computing far beyond entertainment.

Yet, Nvidia's journey was anything but smooth. The company's first product, the NV1, was a commercial failure. It was over-engineered and lacked focus, attempting to do too many things at once. For a lesser entrepreneur, this could have been the end. Investors were hesitant, employees were shaken, and Nvidia faced an existential crisis. But Huang was not in it for short-term success. Instead of retreating, he doubled down, learning from the failure and preparing for the next opportunity.

Huang recognized that technological revolutions did not happen overnight. He believed that if Nvidia kept iterating, learning, and refining its vision, the world would eventually catch up. He was willing to endure the pain of short-term setbacks to build something that could last for decades.

Investing in GPUs Before the Market Understood Their Potential

By the late 1990s, Nvidia had begun to find its footing. The release of the RIVA 128 in 1997 and the GeForce 256 in 1999 marked significant breakthroughs. But Huang was already thinking ahead. He saw GPUs not just as tools for gaming but as computational powerhouses capable of accelerating complex mathematical calculations. While the industry continued to treat GPUs as niche products, Huang envisioned a future where they would be central to scientific computing, artificial intelligence, and data analytics.

This vision led to Nvidia's investment in CUDA (Compute Unified Device Architecture) in 2006. At the time, the idea of using GPUs for general-purpose computing was met with skepticism. Most industry leaders dismissed it as unnecessary, arguing that CPUs would always be sufficient for high-performance computing. But Huang was steadfast. He knew that as data sets grew and computational demands skyrocketed, GPUs would prove indispensable.

It took nearly a decade for CUDA to gain widespread adoption. In the interim, Nvidia poured millions into research and development, building software infrastructure, and convincing developers to experiment with parallel processing on GPUs. There were no immediate financial rewards. There was no guarantee of success. But Huang was not looking for quick returns; he was planting seeds for a future he knew would arrive.

Weathering Industry Shifts and Market Crashes

Throughout Nvidia's history, Huang demonstrated an uncanny ability to endure market downturns without sacrificing long-term vision. In the early 2000s, as the dot-com bubble burst, many tech companies slashed investments, pivoted strategies, or closed down entirely. Nvidia, however, continued to innovate, investing in research while competitors hesitated.

A similar test came in 2008 during the global financial crisis. Demand for graphics cards plummeted as consumers and businesses cut spending. Many companies reacted by scaling back ambitions and focusing on short-term revenue generation. Huang, however, kept Nvidia on its long-term path. Instead of pulling back, he pushed forward, making strategic bets on artificial intelligence and data center computing.

This commitment paid off a decade later when deep learning and AI exploded in popularity. The groundwork Nvidia had laid through CUDA, Tensor Cores, and GPU-accelerated computing positioned it as the undisputed leader in AI hardware. By the time the industry realized the importance of AI, Nvidia had already secured its place at the forefront.

The AI Revolution: Seeing What Others Couldn't

Perhaps the greatest testament to Huang's long-term thinking was Nvidia's role in the AI revolution. In the early 2010s, most technology executives viewed artificial intelligence as a distant dream. While research institutions experimented with machine learning models, few saw it as a commercial opportunity. CPUs dominated data centers, and traditional computing architectures seemed sufficient.

But Huang saw what others missed. He recognized that AI required immense parallel processing power—something GPUs were uniquely suited for. Instead of waiting for market validation, he invested heavily in AI-focused hardware. Nvidia introduced GPUs optimized for deep learning, collaborated with AI researchers, and developed software frameworks like cuDNN to support neural networks.

The turning point came in 2012 when AlexNet, a deep learning model trained using Nvidia GPUs, shattered previous benchmarks in image recognition. Suddenly, the AI community took notice. Researchers, startups, and tech giants flocked to Nvidia's hardware, realizing that GPUs were essential for AI development. What had once been an obscure bet became a multibillion-dollar industry.

Today, Nvidia dominates AI computing. Its chips power everything from self-driving cars to medical research, from language models to climate simulations. This success did not happen overnight. It was the result of over a decade of long-term planning, relentless investment, and unwavering belief in an idea before the world caught up.

Building a Company That Endures

For Huang, playing the long game was not just about technology—it was about culture. He built Nvidia with a philosophy of resilience, adaptability, and relentless curiosity. He instilled in his employees the mindset that short-term failures were stepping stones to long-term success. He maintained a flat organizational structure to ensure fast decision-making and continuous learning.

Perhaps most importantly, he never wavered in his belief that endurance was the key to greatness. As he once put it, "Excellence is the capacity to take pain." Nvidia's journey was filled with obstacles, but each challenge strengthened its foundation.

Today, Nvidia is one of the most valuable technology companies in the world, not because it followed industry trends, but because it set them. The company's success is a testament to Huang's philosophy: that true innovation requires patience, conviction, and a willingness to bet on the future, even when no one else sees it.

As the world moves into the era of AI, quantum computing, and virtual reality, one thing remains certain: Jensen Huang will still be thinking years ahead, playing the long game, and building for a future that others have yet to imagine.

The CEO Who Trolled His Own Fans

Jensen Huang is known for his visionary leadership, relentless innovation, and deep connection with the gaming and AI communities. But he also has a playful side—one that once led him to troll his own company's fans online.

NVIDIA has one of the most dedicated and passionate fanbases in the tech world. Enthusiasts spend hours dissecting every announcement, analyzing leaks, and predicting what the company will do next. The speculation around new GPU releases is particularly intense, with forums filled with theories, supposed insider information, and endless debates about upcoming hardware.

One of these posts caught Jensen Huang's eye. A dedicated fan had written a long, detailed analysis predicting NVIDIA's next GPU lineup. The post was well thought out, citing past trends, leaked benchmarks, and logical assumptions. Other users engaged in the discussion, debating the merits of the speculation and adding their own insights. The thread quickly gained traction, attracting hundreds of replies and widespread attention in the NVIDIA community.

Huang, who frequently keeps an eye on forums and community discussions, couldn't resist. Instead of watching from the sidelines, he decided to step in—anonymously.

Using a fake account, Huang jumped into the conversation. He read through the fan's elaborate breakdown of NVIDIA's future plans and, without offering any details, left a simple comment: "This is completely wrong."

At first, users dismissed the reply as just another contrarian trying to stir controversy. The original poster defended their analysis, and the debate continued. Some users questioned why the comment lacked evidence or reasoning, while others joined in, trying to debunk or support the original speculation.

The thread continued for days, with the cryptic response fueling more speculation. Was it just a random internet troll? A disgruntled former employee? A well-informed industry insider? No one knew. The conversation went viral, spreading across gaming and tech forums, with some even joking that it might be someone from NVIDIA trying to throw them off track.

A few weeks later, the truth came out: the mysterious commenter was none other than Jensen Huang himself. The revelation sent shockwaves through the community. Fans were stunned, amused, and impressed that the CEO of a trillion-dollar company had taken the time to engage in an online debate disguised as an anonymous user.

The internet exploded with reactions. Memes flooded forums and social media, with captions like "Jensen Huang, master of GPUs and trolling," and "CEO by day, internet troll by night." Some users joked about how their speculation had been personally debunked by the man who actually designed the product. Others saw it as a testament to Huang's deep involvement in the gaming world—he wasn't just running the company; he was actively engaged in its community.

When asked about the incident in an interview, Huang laughed and admitted to the prank. "I couldn't help myself," he said. "The analysis was impressive, but I had to keep them guessing. It's part of the fun."

His response only endeared him further to the community. Fans appreciated the fact that their CEO wasn't just some distant executive making corporate decisions—he was one of them. He understood their excitement, their passion, and even their humor.

From that moment on, fans knew that Huang was watching, reading, and sometimes even participating in discussions under the radar. The incident became legendary in NVIDIA circles, with users frequently joking about whether an anonymous comment on a tech forum might secretly be Huang himself.

This wasn't the first time Huang had directly engaged with NVIDIA's fanbase, nor would it be the last. He has a history of personally responding to engineers, researchers, and gamers, whether through emails, social media, or surprise in-person visits. He believes that staying connected to the people who use NVIDIA's technology is critical to the company's success.

But what made this incident stand out was how it showcased his personality. Huang isn't just a corporate leader—he's a tech enthusiast, a gamer, and someone who enjoys being part of the culture NVIDIA has helped shape. He doesn't just oversee product development; he actively follows discussions, appreciates fan theories, and sometimes, just for fun, decides to stir the pot.

To this day, fans still joke about the time they were trolled by their own CEO. The phrase "This is completely wrong" has become an inside joke in NVIDIA communities, often appearing in speculation threads whenever someone makes a bold prediction about future products.

The incident also serves as a reminder of what makes NVIDIA unique. While other companies have distant, inaccessible executives, NVIDIA has a CEO who genuinely enjoys engaging with his community. And if that means occasionally jumping into a forum thread under a fake username just to keep everyone on their toes, so be it.

Jensen Huang's trolling may have been playful, but it also reinforced a larger truth: when it comes to NVIDIA, expect the unexpected. And if you ever find yourself deep in a speculative debate about the company's next move, remember—Huang might just be watching.

Chapter 18: The Teacher Within (CEO)

In another life, Jensen Huang might have been a teacher.

This is the opening line of the book that chronicles his journey, and it is a sentiment that rings true in every aspect of his leadership. Throughout his tenure at Nvidia, Jensen has exemplified the role of a teacher, imparting wisdom, reinforcing principles, and shaping the minds of those who work alongside him. His ability to break down complex ideas into digestible insights has made him more than just a CEO—he is an educator, a mentor, and an architect of knowledge within his organization.

Great founders often see themselves not just as decision-makers, but as teachers who cultivate a culture of excellence. Jensen embodies this philosophy, much like legendary leaders before him—Sol Price, Henry Singleton, Warren Buffett, Bill Walsh, and Steve Jobs—who dedicated much of their time to educating their teams. Jim Sinegal, the founder of Costco, famously said, "If you're not spending 90% of your time teaching as a leader, you're not doing your job." Jensen seems to live by this very principle.

At Nvidia, employees have a nickname for their leader: "Professor Jensen." His meetings are not just strategic discussions; they are classrooms where ideas are dissected, theories are debated, and visions are refined. He continuously reinforces the company's philosophy, ensuring that Nvidia's mission is not just understood but deeply internalized by every employee.

Sol Price once proposed that the best leaders create "alter egos" within their teams. This means that through rigorous teaching and mentorship, a leader empowers employees to perform their jobs as well as, or even better than, the leader himself. Jensen operates with this philosophy, building a workforce that does not just follow orders but thinks, innovates, and executes with a clarity of purpose that mirrors his own.

He does not believe in simply delegating tasks. Instead, he ensures that those he entrusts with responsibilities fully grasp the reasoning, strategy, and execution behind them. This approach has created a company culture where decisions are not just carried out—they are understood, debated, and refined in real-time.

For Jensen, the whiteboard is more than just a tool; it is his preferred battlefield for ideas. While some CEOs rely on lengthy memos or polished presentations, Jensen believes in the power of real-time thinking and collaboration. In countless Nvidia meetings, he is known to leap up with a marker in hand, diagramming a problem or sketching an idea as discussions unfold.

Even when others are speaking, he actively participates, drawing connections, refining thoughts, and pushing the team to think more critically. Whiteboarding, for him, is a real-time stress test of ideas. There is no hiding behind jargon or vagueness—every proposal must withstand the scrutiny of open discussion and visual representation.

The best leaders are evangelists, constantly teaching and reinforcing their vision. Jensen is no exception. His teaching extends beyond meetings and strategy sessions; it is woven into the very fabric of Nvidia's DNA. He has shaped the company into an extension of himself, much like how Steve Jobs once said that Apple was "Steve Jobs with 10,000 lives."

Jensen's employees share his singular focus on Nvidia's mission, his relentless work ethic, and his insatiable drive to outpace the competition. He has embedded in them a philosophy of constant learning and high performance, ensuring that his vision for Nvidia continues long after he has left the room.

Jensen Huang's story is not just one of technological breakthroughs and business success—it is a testament to the power of teaching. His ability to educate, inspire, and elevate those around him has been a defining force in Nvidia's rise. In every lesson he imparts, in every whiteboard session he leads, and in every principle he reinforces, he solidifies his place not just as a CEO, but as one of the great teachers of the modern business world.

A Student of the Future

Jensen Huang never stopped being a student. Even as the CEO of Nvidia, one of the most powerful technology companies in the world, he carried with him a relentless curiosity that set him apart. While many leaders relied on instinct or delegated learning to specialists, Jensen immersed himself in knowledge, constantly seeking new ideas, absorbing lessons from history, and staying ahead of technological shifts before they became obvious to the world. He did not believe that a leader should simply manage; he believed that a leader must understand—deeply and personally.

It was a principle instilled in him from an early age. When Jensen was a child, his mother, realizing the importance of English in their future, assigned him ten words from the dictionary every day. He was required to memorize, spell, and use them in sentences. It was an exercise in discipline, but more importantly, it was an exercise in the habit of learning—an approach that Jensen would refine throughout his life. His formative years at the Oneida

Baptist Institute, where he and his brother were mistakenly sent under the assumption that it was a prestigious prep school, only reinforced this idea. The school was rigorous, demanding both physical and intellectual endurance. It was here that Jensen learned resilience, but he also learned to study his environment, to adapt, and to absorb information rapidly.

By the time he entered the world of semiconductors, working at AMD and later at LSI Logic, he had already adopted an unrelenting hunger for knowledge. Unlike many engineers who specialized in narrow fields, Jensen took an expansive approach. He sought to understand not only chip design but the entire ecosystem—how products were manufactured, how they were sold, and how the technology landscape was shifting globally. While at LSI Logic, he paid close attention to his interactions with Sun Microsystems, not just as a business relationship but as an educational experience. Every meeting, every product launch, every shift in corporate strategy was an opportunity to learn.

Jensen's curiosity was not limited to the technical aspects of his work. He was just as eager to learn about business strategy, leadership, and market dynamics. When he and his co-founders started Nvidia, he immersed himself in every available resource on running a company. He sought out advice from seasoned executives, read books on business and innovation, and absorbed lessons from the successes and failures of other companies. One of his greatest influences was Charlie Munger, the vice chairman of Berkshire Hathaway, whose philosophies on mental models and multidisciplinary thinking resonated deeply with him. Munger's belief in the power of combining knowledge from multiple fields aligned perfectly with Jensen's approach.

Even as Nvidia became successful, Jensen never allowed himself to become complacent. He maintained the mindset of a student, always seeking out experts in emerging fields. When artificial intelligence began gaining traction, he didn't wait for the market to dictate its relevance—he studied it himself. He attended academic conferences, engaged directly with researchers, and immersed himself in the details of AI's potential applications. Unlike many executives who relied solely on their research and development teams to filter information, Jensen was in the trenches, learning alongside them.

His ability to learn quickly and synthesize information into actionable strategy became one of Nvidia's greatest competitive advantages. When the company pivoted from being primarily a gaming graphics card manufacturer to becoming a dominant force in AI computing, it wasn't just a strategic shift—it was the direct result of Jensen's education. He had studied the needs of AI researchers, recognized the limitations of existing computing architectures, and understood how Nvidia's parallel processing capabilities could be applied to deep learning. His learning wasn't passive; it was deeply connected to action.

Jensen's commitment to learning extended beyond just technological trends. He studied leadership meticulously, refining his own approach based on insights from historical figures and contemporary executives. He admired the precision and intensity of Steve Jobs, the relentless efficiency of Jeff Bezos, and the disciplined decision-making of Warren Buffett. But he never imitated them outright. Instead, he took their lessons and adapted them to his own philosophy. He believed that the best way to learn was to integrate knowledge into one's own identity rather than mimic others.

Even in his daily routines, learning was embedded into his life. Jensen was known for engaging in deep, intellectually rigorous discussions with Nvidia's top engineers and executives. Meetings often turned into impromptu lectures, where he would challenge his team to think critically and approach problems from new angles. He was famous for his use of the whiteboard, where he would diagram complex ideas in real-time, forcing those around him to engage in the learning process with him. "At the whiteboard," he often said, "there is no place to hide."

He also had a habit of absorbing knowledge from unexpected places. Unlike many CEOs who were insulated from ground-level conversations, Jensen regularly spoke with junior engineers, researchers, and even customers. He wanted to understand firsthand what challenges they faced, what innovations excited them, and what gaps in technology needed to be filled. This was not just a leadership tactic—it was an extension of his lifelong commitment to learning.

One of his most well-known qualities was his ability to anticipate industry shifts long before they happened. This was not due to luck or guesswork but because he had already immersed himself in studying the forces shaping the future. When Nvidia doubled down on AI and data centers, competitors were still focused on traditional computing markets. By the time the rest of the industry caught up, Nvidia had already established itself as the leader. Jensen's ability to learn, adapt, and act with conviction set the company apart.

But Jensen's learning wasn't confined to his professional life. He was an avid reader, absorbing books across a range of disciplines, from history and philosophy to physics and economics. He believed that the best insights often came from outside one's field and that drawing connections between seemingly unrelated topics was where true innovation happened. He once remarked that some of the most important lessons for Nvidia had come not from tech industry case studies but from unexpected sources, like military history or biology.

As Nvidia grew into one of the most valuable companies in the world, Jensen's commitment to continuous learning remained unchanged. While some CEOs became detached from the day-to-day realities of their industries, Jensen remained a student of the future. He understood that the world was changing too fast for any leader to rely on past knowledge alone. The only way to stay ahead was to keep learning, to remain curious, and to never assume that one had all the answers.

For Jensen, learning was not a phase of life—it was a lifelong discipline. It was a force that had guided him from a young immigrant boy memorizing dictionary words to the CEO of a company that was shaping the future of computing. It was his greatest strength, the engine behind Nvidia's success, and the principle that ensured he was never left behind.

Even as he stood at the pinnacle of the technology world, Jensen Huang remained, above all else, a student.

NVIDIA's Secretive Black Ops Retreat

Every great company has its rituals—traditions that bring together its brightest minds to shape the future. For NVIDIA, this ritual is an annual off-site retreat so secretive that even employees outside the inner circle don't know where it takes place or what is discussed. Jensen Huang, the company's visionary CEO, calls it the "black ops" retreat, a name fitting for a company that thrives on stealth innovation and cutting-edge breakthroughs.

This exclusive gathering is not a mere corporate retreat filled with team-building exercises and motivational speeches. It is a high-stakes, high-intensity strategy session where the most important decisions about NVIDIA's future are made. Only the top executives and key decision-makers are invited. The purpose? To brainstorm, debate, and refine the company's vision for the years ahead.

Huang is known for his deep involvement in NVIDIA's direction, and this retreat is his way of ensuring that the company never falls behind. He has always believed that true innovation doesn't happen in boardrooms filled with PowerPoint slides and scripted presentations. It happens when a small, brilliant group of people is given the freedom to think outside the constraints of day-to-day operations and imagine what the future could look like.

The secrecy surrounding the retreat is part of what makes it so fascinating. Unlike other tech giants, which often publicize their leadership retreats or shareholder meetings, NVIDIA keeps its "black ops" trip completely under wraps. There are no press releases, no leaks, and no official records of what takes place. Employees who attend are sworn to confidentiality, adding an aura of mystery to the event.

Where do they go? The locations vary year by year, but they are always chosen with two key factors in mind: isolation and inspiration. Past attendees have hinted at everything from remote mountain lodges to secluded coastal retreats. The goal is to disconnect from the outside world and create an environment where deep thinking and bold ideas can flourish.

Once the group arrives at the undisclosed location, the real work begins. The retreat is structured but flexible. Huang encourages open dialogue, challenging his executives to question assumptions and push the boundaries of what's possible. Sessions often revolve around major technological trends, shifts in the market, and internal challenges NVIDIA must overcome.

One of the most remarkable aspects of these retreats is how many of NVIDIA's groundbreaking innovations have been born in these meetings. The decision to pivot from gaming GPUs to AI acceleration? That was reportedly first debated at one of these gatherings. The bold investment in CUDA, which transformed GPUs into a critical tool for deep learning? Another brainchild of a black ops session. Even the company's push into autonomous vehicles and data centers can be traced back to ideas refined during these retreats.

Huang's approach to these off-sites is intense, but it's also deeply collaborative. He doesn't just want his executives to agree with him—he wants them to challenge him. "The best ideas come from friction," he has said. "If we all think the same way, we're not thinking big enough." This philosophy drives the discussions at the retreat, where debates can be as heated as they are productive.

Unlike conventional corporate retreats that focus on short-term strategy, the black ops meetings are about NVIDIA's long-term trajectory. Where will AI be in five years? What role will GPUs play in the next decade? What technological shifts are happening that the company needs to anticipate before anyone else does? These are the kinds of questions that shape the agenda.

Despite the secrecy, the impact of these meetings is clear. Every year, following the retreat, NVIDIA emerges with a clearer sense of direction, a renewed commitment to innovation, and, more often than not, an ambitious new initiative that propels the company even further ahead of its competition. Employees who aren't part of the inner circle may not know what happens at these gatherings, but they feel the effects in the form of bold new projects and aggressive strategic moves.

Perhaps what makes the black ops retreat so powerful is that it embodies

Huang's leadership style—intensely focused, highly strategic, and always looking ahead. While other companies might rely on incremental progress, NVIDIA thrives on disruptive leaps. And those leaps often begin in an undisclosed location, where a handful of brilliant minds gather to map out the future.

As NVIDIA continues to lead in AI, gaming, and computing, one thing remains certain: somewhere in the world, once a year, a secret meeting is taking place, shaping the technology that will define the next decade. And at the center of it all is Jensen Huang, orchestrating the next great leap forward for NVIDIA.

Chapter 19: Obsession with Talent

As the world ground to a halt in early 2020, uncertainty gripped nearly every industry. Companies scrambled to adjust to the pandemic, cutting costs, laying off employees, and in some cases, shutting down entirely. It was a time of fear and instability, and for many workers, the sudden shift to remote work only deepened the anxiety. Amid this chaos, Jensen Huang did something that would become legendary within Nvidia.

Instead of focusing on losses or engaging in damage control like many other CEOs, Huang sat down and wrote a letter—a personal, heartfelt message to every single Nvidia employee. It wasn't a memo filled with corporate jargon or a carefully crafted PR statement. It was raw, honest, and deeply human.

Jensen's message was simple: Nvidia was not going to abandon its people.

He acknowledged the hardships that everyone was facing, from the struggles of working from home to the fear of an uncertain future. He reminded them that their work mattered, not just to Nvidia, but to the world. The technologies they were building—AI, graphics processing, and computing power—were helping researchers find solutions, assisting healthcare professionals, and keeping the world connected.

Most importantly, he made it clear that Nvidia was not going to lay off employees due to the crisis. While many other companies were resorting to job cuts to survive, Jensen reassured his team that they were part of something bigger. Nvidia would weather the storm together, and no one would be left behind.

This letter, meant simply as an internal note, quickly took on a life of its own. Employees shared it with friends and family. It was quoted in industry articles and business forums. People outside Nvidia read it and marveled at how different it was from the impersonal, calculated responses other corporations were issuing. It became a beacon of hope and an example of leadership rooted in empathy rather than fear.

For many Nvidia employees, it was a defining moment. The company's stock had taken a hit, projects were delayed, and the future was unpredictable, but that letter reinforced what had always been at the core of Nvidia's culture—trust, resilience, and the belief that great companies are built on great people.

Jensen's approach paid off. While some tech giants struggled to regain momentum after the initial shock of the pandemic, Nvidia emerged stronger than ever. The company adapted quickly, empowering employees to innovate from home, streamlining collaboration, and finding new ways to push forward.

By the time the world began to recover, Nvidia had not only survived but thrived. It had expanded its dominance in AI, gaming, and data centers, proving that a company that stands by its people will always find a way forward.

Years later, the letter remains a part of Nvidia's internal history—a testament to the power of leadership in times of crisis. It wasn't just about protecting jobs; it was about showing employees that they mattered, that their work had purpose, and that their leader believed in them even in the darkest of times.

Jensen never saw the letter as anything extraordinary. To him, it was simply the right thing to do. But for those who received it, it was a moment they would never forget, a moment when their CEO reminded them that at Nvidia, they were more than just employees—they were a family.

Rejecting the Ordinary

Jensen Huang never set out to build just another technology company. From the very beginning, his vision for Nvidia was different—not about competition, but about creation. He was not interested in market share battles or incremental improvements; he wanted to build something unique, something that had never been done before.

"Our company decides to choose projects for one fundamental goal," he explained in a speech, articulating a belief that had guided him from the earliest days of Nvidia. "My goal is to create an amazing environment for the best people in the world who want to pursue this field of computing and artificial intelligence—to create the conditions by which they will come and do their life's work."

For Jensen, innovation was not just about building products; it was about attracting the right minds, giving them the freedom to pursue groundbreaking ideas, and ensuring they had the patience and endurance to bring those ideas to life.

But how does a company achieve this?

Jensen believed that the surest way to drive away great talent was to engage in uninspiring work. He had no interest in copying competitors, fighting for existing markets, or making minor improvements to established technologies.

"Nobody that I know wakes up in the morning and says, 'You know what my neighbor is doing? I want to take it from them. I want to capture their share. I want to pummel them on price,'" he said. "No great people do that."

Instead, great minds seek challenges. They want to do something that has never been done before, something incredibly hard, something that—if successful—will have a massive impact on the world. This, Jensen insisted, was Nvidia's guiding philosophy.

"We choose to do something that the world's never done before. Let's hope that it's insanely hard to do. If that's the case, what am I doing making a cell phone chip? How many companies in the world can make a cell phone chip? A lot. Why am I making a CPU? How many more CPUs do we need?"

For Nvidia, the answer was clear: avoid commodity markets, avoid replication, and focus only on creating the impossible.

The Power of Choosing the Right Problems

Jensen understood that talent follows ambition. The best engineers in the world do not flock to companies that make incremental improvements; they are drawn to places where they can push boundaries.

"Because we selected amazing markets, amazingly hard things to do, amazing people joined us," he explained. "And because amazing people joined us—and because we had the patience to let them do something amazing—they did something amazing."

This was the Nvidia formula: find a problem that no one else had solved, bring in the best minds to tackle it, and give them the space to work. It was, in many ways, a deceptively simple idea, but it required an extraordinary level of discipline to execute.

Jensen emphasized that patience was crucial. True innovation took time, and companies that chased quick wins or followed market trends rarely built anything revolutionary.

"It turns out it's simple to say," he admitted. "It takes incredible character to do."

The Art of Knowing What Not to Do

Equally important to Jensen's philosophy was knowing when not to compete. He saw no value in wasting resources on problems that had already been solved or industries where competition was about price rather than innovation.

For example, Nvidia did not enter the semiconductor fabrication business, despite the company's deep expertise in chip design. The reason? Taiwan Semiconductor Manufacturing Company (TSMC) already did it exceptionally well.

"The reason why we don't do fabrication is because TSMC does it so well," Jensen explained. "And they're already doing it. For what reason do I go take their work? I like the people at TSMC. They're great friends of mine. Just because I've got business I can drive into it? So what? They're doing a great job for me."

Rather than replicating what already existed, Jensen insisted on directing Nvidia's energy toward entirely new challenges.

"Let's not squander my time to go repeat what they've already done. Let's go squander my time on something that nobody has done."

For him, that was the key to building something truly special.

The Jensen Huang Way

Jensen's approach to innovation—choosing the hardest problems, avoiding commodity markets, and fostering an environment where exceptional people could do exceptional work—became the foundation of Nvidia's success.

He was never interested in playing the same game as everyone else. He wanted to redefine the game entirely.

That mindset attracted the world's best engineers, led to the development of groundbreaking technologies, and cemented Nvidia's position as one of the most innovative companies in the world.

In the end, Jensen Huang's philosophy could be summed up in one simple idea:

"Otherwise, you're only talking about market share."

And for him, market share was never the goal. The goal was to build the future.

If there is one principle that defines Jensen Huang's leadership at Nvidia, it is his relentless pursuit of exceptional talent. From the company's earliest days, he has believed that the right people are the foundation of success, and he has built Nvidia with an unwavering commitment to hiring, developing, and retaining the best minds in the world.

Unlike many Silicon Valley companies that expand rapidly and frequently lay off employees, Nvidia takes a different approach. Huang rarely fires people, and even more remarkably, employees rarely choose to leave. In an industry where attrition rates often exceed 17%, Nvidia's turnover rate is an astonishingly low 2.7%.

For Huang, talent is not just about skill—it is about mindset, endurance, and the ability to thrive in an environment of relentless pressure and high expectations. He has created a company culture where only the most resilient and driven individuals survive, and where the rewards for those who do are immense.

The Relentless Pursuit of the Best

Huang's hiring philosophy is built on one simple belief: the difference between an average employee and a great one is not incremental—it is exponential.

"I think that the interview process is not an excellent way to judge whether somebody is a good fit," Huang said in an episode of the Tech Unheard podcast. "I mean, obviously, everybody could pretend to have a very constructive conversation."

In other words, technical skills alone are not enough. Candidates can prepare for interviews, memorize the right answers, and present a polished version of themselves. But what they cannot change is their history—the impact they have had in previous roles, the reputation they have built, and the way they have been perceived by those who have worked alongside them.

That is why Huang places far greater emphasis on reference checks than on the interview itself.

"My method is always I go back to reference checks and I ask them the questions that I was going to ask the candidate," he explained. "And the reason for that is you could always make for a great moment, but it's hard for you to run away from your past."

In other words, an interview is a performance, but a candidate's track record is real. By speaking to former colleagues and managers, Huang gets a clearer picture of the person he is considering hiring—not just their technical capabilities, but their work ethic, their problem-solving skills, and their ability to thrive under pressure.

This rigorous selection process has ensured that Nvidia's workforce is made up of people who are not just competent, but extraordinary.

For those who make it through the hiring process, life at Nvidia is not easy. The company operates at an intensity level that few others can match, and the pressure to perform is relentless.

A Bloomberg report that cited multiple current and former Nvidia employees described the work atmosphere as a "pressure cooker," with meetings often stretching past 2 a.m. and discussions punctuated by intense debates, yelling, and fierce competition.

This culture is not accidental—it is by design.

Huang has always believed that greatness is forged in adversity, and he has deliberately cultivated an environment where only the most dedicated individuals can thrive. At Nvidia, employees are expected to push themselves to their absolute limits, to work harder and smarter than they ever have before, and to constantly challenge themselves and those around them.

Those who cannot handle the intensity either leave or are pushed out. But for those who do survive, the rewards are immense. Nvidia's explosive growth in recent years has made many long-term employees wealthy, and the company's stock has continued to climb as demand for its products, including its highly anticipated Blackwell AI chip, has skyrocketed.

Huang is not interested in creating a comfortable workplace. He is interested in building a company that changes the world. And that requires people who are not just talented, but relentless.

Why Nvidia Employees Rarely Leave

Despite the grueling work hours and intense expectations, Nvidia employees tend to stay for the long haul.

The company's culture is built on more than just pressure—it is built on purpose. Employees are not just working long hours for the sake of working long hours. They are building groundbreaking technology, solving some of the hardest problems in the world, and working alongside some of the most brilliant minds in the industry.

For many, this is more than just a job—it is a mission.

Huang has cultivated an environment where employees feel a deep sense of ownership over their work. They are not just cogs in a machine; they are driving the future of AI, gaming, and high-performance computing. And because the hiring process is so selective, those who do make it in know that they are part of an elite group—one that is capable of achieving things that no other company in the world can match.

At Nvidia, the expectation is not just to do your job, but to redefine what is possible.

And that is why the people who work there stay.

Huang's obsession with talent is not just about hiring the right people—it is about creating an environment where only the best can thrive.

He has built Nvidia into a company that does not settle for mediocrity. There are no easy jobs, no free passes, and no tolerance for complacency. Employees are expected to push themselves beyond their limits, to think bigger, to work harder, and to never stop improving.

This is not a company for everyone. But for those who can meet the challenge, it is the opportunity of a lifetime.

As Huang himself puts it:

"If you're looking for comfort, you're in the wrong place. But if you want to build things that change the world, welcome to Nvidia."

And for those who make it through the crucible, the rewards are worth it.

NVIDIA

Chapter 20: The Power of Recognition

Jensen Huang had always believed that leadership was not just about setting the vision and making decisions but about acknowledging the people who made those decisions possible. From Nvidia's earliest days, he ensured that recognition was a core part of the company's DNA. He was acutely aware that innovation was not a solitary act but a collective effort, and he wanted everyone at Nvidia to feel valued for their contributions. His method of recognizing achievements, however, was not formulaic or superficial—it was deeply personal, thoughtful, and intentional.

Huang did not believe in generic praise. A simple "good job" was never his style. Instead, he took the time to understand the nuances of each project, each milestone, and each breakthrough. When someone at Nvidia contributed meaningfully, he ensured that the recognition was as precise as the work itself.

For instance, when the team successfully launched the first GeForce GPU, it was a monumental achievement. The engineering team had worked tirelessly to bring an ambitious concept to life, and Huang wanted to celebrate them in a way that resonated. He didn't just call for a company-wide meeting to offer words of encouragement—he took the time to highlight individual engineers, describing their contributions in technical detail. He understood that the engineers didn't just want applause; they wanted their hard work and ingenuity to be seen and understood. Huang delivered exactly that, reinforcing a culture where effort never went unnoticed.

This practice became even more pronounced as Nvidia grew. With thousands of employees, it would have been easy for leadership to become detached from individual contributions. But Huang remained committed to making recognition an essential part of Nvidia's culture. He would walk into engineering labs unannounced, ask about the latest challenges, and, when breakthroughs happened, ensure that credit was given where it was due. This not only boosted morale but also encouraged an environment where innovation flourished.

The Role of Public Recognition

While Huang was known for his personal acknowledgments, he also understood the power of public recognition. He often used Nvidia's major events—whether internal or external—to shine a light on the people behind the technology. At major product launches, he would share the stage with the engineers and designers who had made the impossible possible, ensuring that their work was not just a footnote but the highlight of the presentation.

During Nvidia's transition to AI-driven computing, a critical shift in the company's trajectory, Huang knew that the teams working on AI models and software optimization were solving problems that few in the industry had even begun to consider. At the annual GTC (GPU Technology Conference), instead of solely discussing the company's future plans, he devoted a significant portion of his keynote to celebrating the engineers who had pushed the boundaries of AI computing. He named them, detailed their challenges, and shared stories of late-night debugging sessions that led to groundbreaking advancements. It was not just a speech—it was a testament to the people who made Nvidia what it was.

This approach had a profound effect. It reinforced the idea that Nvidia was not just a company but a community of innovators where every contribution mattered. Employees knew that their work would not disappear into the corporate machine but would be recognized and appreciated at the highest levels.

While public acknowledgment was impactful, Huang also believed in the power of private recognition. He had a habit of personally reaching out to employees who had made exceptional contributions. This could be through a direct email, a handwritten note, or even a surprise visit to their workspace.

One famous instance of this came after the successful launch of Nvidia's CUDA platform. CUDA was a revolutionary technology that transformed how GPUs were used, expanding their capabilities far beyond graphics into scientific computing, AI, and deep learning. The engineers who had worked on CUDA had done so against skepticism from the industry, and Huang knew the toll it had taken. Instead of a standard congratulatory message, he personally visited the core CUDA team, sat down with them, and discussed the journey. He asked about their struggles, their moments of doubt, and their breakthroughs. Then, he thanked each of them individually, not just for what they had built but for the resilience they had shown.

Employees often recalled these moments as defining experiences in their careers. It wasn't just about the recognition itself but about how genuine it felt. Huang made people feel seen, not just as engineers or employees, but as individuals whose dedication had real impact.

Huang was also a firm believer in recognizing potential, not just achievement. He had an eye for talent and made it a point to elevate rising stars within the company. He often challenged young engineers, giving them responsibilities that seemed beyond their years but offering guidance along the way. When they succeeded, he made sure their work was acknowledged in front of the company, reinforcing the idea that growth and opportunity were central to Nvidia's culture.

One such example was an intern who had contributed significantly to an optimization problem in Nvidia's deep learning frameworks. Instead of simply commending the intern privately, Huang made sure the intern's contribution was acknowledged in front of senior engineers. That intern later became a full-time employee and rose through the ranks, crediting Huang's recognition as a pivotal moment in his career.

Huang's approach to recognition wasn't just about boosting morale—it had strategic implications. It created a culture where employees were driven not just by salaries or bonuses but by a sense of purpose and belonging. It instilled a mindset where people took ownership of their work, knowing that if they did something extraordinary, it would be acknowledged.

It also shaped how Nvidia operated as a company. Unlike many large corporations where contributions often go unnoticed, Nvidia developed a culture where employees were deeply invested in their projects. They knew that their work mattered, and that Jensen Huang himself would take notice.

As Nvidia continued to push the boundaries of technology, Huang's leadership philosophy remained unchanged. He understood that while technology evolves, the fundamental principles of motivation and leadership do not. People want to be part of something greater than themselves, and they want to know that their efforts are meaningful. By consistently recognizing contributions—big and small—Huang ensured that Nvidia was not just a workplace but a place where innovation was celebrated and the people behind it were honored.

In the annals of technology history, Nvidia's success will be attributed to its groundbreaking innovations, but behind every GPU, every AI breakthrough, and every computational revolution, there are people. And thanks to Jensen Huang, those people never go unnoticed.

A Taste of the Past

Jensen Huang has come a long way from his college days, but some things haven't changed. Despite running one of the most powerful tech companies in the world and being worth billions, he remains deeply connected to the humble, everyday experiences that shaped him. One of the clearest examples of this is his unshakable loyalty to the small, unassuming restaurants that fed him during his student years. For Jensen, these places are more than just eateries; they are reminders of where he came from and the people who helped him along the way.

Long before he was leading Nvidia, Jensen was a struggling student at Oregon State University. Like many college students, he didn't have the luxury of fine dining. Instead, he and his friends relied on affordable, no-frills diners and small noodle shops, places that served hearty meals at a price students could afford. The flavors, the atmosphere, and the camaraderie built around these meals became an essential part of his formative years.

Even after achieving monumental success, Jensen never abandoned these old habits. When he travels for work or visits old friends, he doesn't opt for high-end restaurants or exclusive venues. Instead, he insists on returning to those same small diners and noodle shops he frequented in his youth. These places, often family-owned and unchanged for decades, hold a kind of authenticity that resonates deeply with him.

His old friends and colleagues know that when Jensen is in town, there's no need for reservations at an upscale restaurant. He's far more likely to suggest meeting at an old favorite, a place where the menu is the same as it was decades ago, the portions are generous, and the owners still recognize him when he walks through the door.

One of his most beloved spots is a small noodle shop near his college campus. The place has barely changed since the days when he was a student: the same cracked vinyl booths, the same handwritten menu taped to the wall, and the same owner who still remembers his usual order. He doesn't just eat there for nostalgia—he genuinely believes that the food remains some of the best he's ever had, despite all the Michelin-starred restaurants he's been to over the years.

Jensen's attachment to these humble restaurants is more than just a personal quirk—it's a reflection of his values. While many billionaires embrace extravagant lifestyles and leave their pasts behind, Jensen remains grounded in the experiences that shaped him. He has never let wealth dictate his sense of identity. Instead, he holds on to the things that truly matter: the relationships, the traditions, and the simple joys of a good meal shared with good company.

His insistence on eating at these places also reveals something deeper about his leadership style. At Nvidia, he is known for his hands-on approach, his ability to stay connected to employees at every level, and his belief in the importance of fundamentals. Just as he remains loyal to the food that sustained him in his youth, he remains committed to the core principles that built Nvidia—innovation, perseverance, and a focus on real, meaningful progress rather than unnecessary extravagance.

Employees and colleagues who have dined with him are often struck by how unpretentious he is. There is no grand performance, no effort to impress anyone. He eats with enthusiasm, often chatting with the restaurant owners as if no time has passed since his college days. He appreciates the familiarity, the simplicity, and the continuity of these places in a world that is constantly changing.

Even when dining at high-profile events or industry gatherings, he remains unimpressed by overly complex dishes. He values food that is straightforward, well-made, and comforting. When given the choice, he would rather have a steaming bowl of noodles from a tiny shop than a meticulously plated, overpriced meal at an exclusive restaurant.

For those who know Jensen well, this habit is emblematic of his approach to life. He is a billionaire who never lost sight of what truly makes him happy. He doesn't seek luxury for the sake of status. Instead, he seeks authenticity, whether in the technology he develops, the people he surrounds himself with, or the meals he eats.

His love for these small restaurants is also a lesson in humility. No matter how successful he becomes, he never forgets the struggles of his early years. He understands that the world he inhabits now is vastly different from the one he came from, but he chooses to stay connected to it in tangible ways. His continued patronage of these places is not just about nostalgia—it's about respect for the past and an appreciation for the simple things that bring joy.

In an industry filled with excess and opulence, Jensen Huang stands apart. His legacy is built not just on groundbreaking technology but on an unwavering commitment to his roots. And perhaps, in the quiet moments of enjoying a familiar meal in a tiny, unassuming diner, he finds a reminder of why he started this journey in the first place.

After all, success is not just about where you end up—it's also about remembering where you came from.

Get Your Free Audiobook!

Scan the QR code below to instantly access the audiobook version of this book, absolutely free.

SCAN ME